The Invisible Mountain

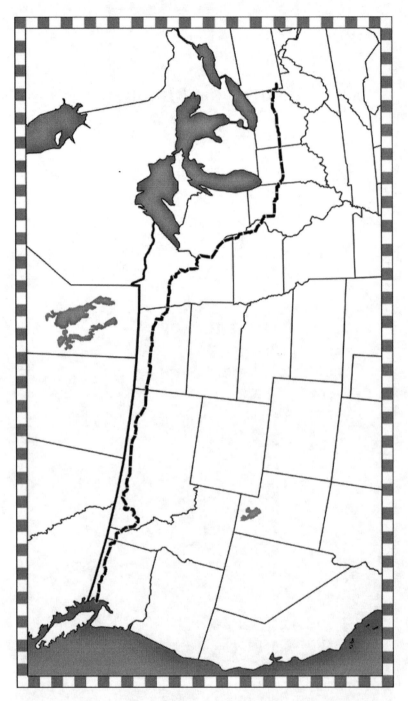

The Northern Tier: Anacortes, Washington to Washington, Pennsylvania

The Invisible Mountain

A Journey of Faith

Robert P. Vande Kappelle

RESOURCE *Publications* · Eugene, Oregon

Resource Publications
An Imprint of Wipf and Stock Publishers
199 W. 8th Ave., Suite 3
Eugene, OR 97401
www.wipfandstock.com

ISBN 13: 978-1-60899-860-9

Bible quotations, unless otherwise noted, are from the *Revised Standard Version of the Bible*, copyright © 1946, 1952, 1971 by the Division of Christian Education of the National Council of the Churches of Christ in the United States of America. Used by permission.

Scripture quotations marked "NIV" are taken from *The Holy Bible, New International Version*, copyright © 1978 by New York International Bible Society.

Scripture quotations from *The Message*. Copyright © by Eugene H. Peterson 1993, 1994, 1995, 1996, 2000, 2001, 2002. Used by permission of NavPress Publishing Group.

Scripture quotations marked "J.B. Phillips" are taken from *The New Testament in Modern English*, copyright © 1958 by Macmillan Inc, now under control of Simon & Schuster. Used by permission.

The lyrics for the jingle "The RAGBRAI Special," used to promote the Register's Annual Great Bicycle Ride Across Iowa, are not copyrighted. They are, however, used by permission of The Des Moines Register.

The Foreword, written by Millard Fuller, is used by permission of the Millard Fuller estate. No part may be used or reproduced in any manner without written permission.

Maps used in this book were created exclusively for *The Invisible Mountain* by William A. ("Will") Burrows.

Cover photo taken by Susan E. Vande Kappelle.

Manufactured in the U.S.A.

To Delbert Wayne Armstrong
(1939–2010)

The poor and the hungry
got poorer and hungrier
the day Wayne died.
—Byron Smialek

The Road of Life

At first, I saw God as my observer, my judge, keeping track of the things I did wrong, so as to know whether I merited heaven or hell when I die. God was out there sort of like a president. I recognized God's picture when I saw it, but I really didn't know God.

Later on in life, when I met God, it seemed as though life were rather like a bike ride, but it was a tandem bike, a bicycle built for two, and I noticed that God was in the back helping me pedal.

I don't know just when it was that God suggested we change places, but my life has not been the same since. When I had control, I knew the way. It was rather boring, but predictable. It was the shortest distance between two points.

But when God took the lead, God knew delightful long cuts, up mountains, and through rocky places at breakneck speeds; it was all I could do to hang on! Even though it looked like madness, God said, "Pedal!"

I was worried and was anxious and asked, "Where are you taking me?" God laughed and didn't answer, and I started to learn to trust. I forgot my boring life and entered into the adventure. And when I'd say, "I'm scared," God would lean back and touch my hand.

God took me to people with gifts that I needed, gifts of healing, acceptance and joy. They gave me gifts to take on my journey, my Lord's and mine. And we were off again. God said, "Give the gifts away; they're extra baggage, too much weight." So I gave them away, to the people we met. And I found that in giving I received; and still our burden was light.

I did not trust God, at first, in control of my life. I thought God would wreck it; but God knows bike secrets, knows how to make it bend to take sharp corners, knows how to jump to clear high rocks, knows how to fly to shorten scary passages.

And I'm learning to shut up and pedal in the strangest places, and I'm beginning to enjoy the view and the cool breeze on my face with my delightful constant companion, God. And when I'm sure I just can't do anymore, God just smiles and says . . . "Pedal."

—author unknown

All of God's people should have at
least a simple, decent place to live.

—Millard Fuller

Consider it pure joy, my brothers,
whenever you face trials of many kinds,
because you know that the testing of your faith
develops perseverance. Perseverance must finish
its work so that you may be mature and complete,
not lacking anything.

—James 1:2–4 (NIV)

If you want to get from one ocean to the other in this country, you can go by jet in six hours, by car in six days, by
bicycle in six weeks, or by foot in six months. If you take the
jet, you remain a total stranger to the land. The car . . . still
keeps you too much a spectator . . . But with the bicycle . . .
America becomes your intimate companion.

—Barbara Stedman

Contents

Rev. Roe, Bob Vande Kappelle, Millard Fuller, Susan Vande Kappelle

Foreword

THIS IS A GOOD book—good because it is exciting, relevant, and keeps moving. Once you start reading, it's hard to put down.

The Invisible Mountain is about all kinds of things—bicycles, houses, a bit of history, one man's courage and determination to go beyond the ordinary to do something for himself and for others. In a way it is a simple story, easy to comprehend, but there is also deep stuff here.

Bob Vande Kappelle went on a journey of faith as he rode his bicycle across the United States to raise money for Habitat for Humanity. Ride with him as you read. You will enjoy the trip and you will gain all sorts of insights into bicycling, faith, human nature, Habitat for Humanity, the Northern Tier of the United States, and perhaps most importantly, you will learn about yourself and grow spiritually as you experience vicariously the wonderful adventure of this "journey of faith."

Millard Fuller
Co-founder
Habitat for Humanity International, Inc.
The Fuller Center for Housing

Acknowledgments

THE ABSENCE OF FICTIONAL characters in this book means that many people need to be thanked. Although I cannot possibly acknowledge everyone, I must begin with Wayne Armstrong, whose vision, energy, and support for the trek made this cycling venture possible. He acquainted me with Habitat for Humanity and was the first to translate my dream of a cross-country cycling trip into an opportunity to help disadvantaged citizens. Wayne coordinated all matters pertaining to the trek, serving as publicity chairman, treasurer, and anything else that was required. He introduced me to Gary Nicholls, Wayne Luther, Bob and Maudie Armstrong, and many others who helped organize the Washington County chapter of Habitat for Humanity. Each of these individuals played an indispensable role in the trek's success. As chairman of the trek, Wayne contacted the headquarters of Habitat for Humanity International, eliciting Habitat's enthusiastic support.

I could not have written the memorial essay at the conclusion of the book without the help of Peggy Armstrong, who provided details of Wayne's life and the moving account of his death. Also indispensable were the members of the Fourth Presbyterian Church of Washington, Pennsylvania. They were there at the beginning, providing financial and emotional support, and they were there at the end, physically present for the homecoming ceremony at the courthouse.

My thanks extend to the hundreds of individuals in Washington County, many of whom contributed the partnership amount of $34 or more, who followed updates of the trek at local malls and through announcements on the WJPA radio station. Pete Povich provided radio exposure and Byron Smialek covered the trek in his newspaper column for the *Observer-Reporter*.

Many individuals across the country embraced the cause, enabling me to go "Homeless for Habitat." Special thanks go to those who provided extraordinary hospitality on behalf of a stranger, a lone cyclist who appeared abruptly and left as a friend, in some cases as an honorary member of the family. The following list includes individuals who may have relocated or are deceased, so I list them by location in 1989: Bob and Carolyn Lehman and Rev. George Tolman in Kalispell, Sharon Clawson in Havre, and Rev. Jim and Bonnie Coats in Wolf Point—all in the "Big Sky Country" of Montana. I will always treasure the stellar support of Clarence and Fern Rau in Williston, North Dakota, for they helped me get back on track when the trek was in jeopardy. At Cooperstown, North Dakota, I met Janice Johnson. The account of her family's perseverance against overwhelming odds is told in chapter 9. Her courage and faith were inspirational and led to a heartwarming visit with Carolyn and Curtis Haugen in Fargo. Their hospitality at the trek's midpoint also included hosting Wayne Armstrong, whose presence at that critical point was vital.

Others who took risks and provided generous support as I traveled America's "Northern Tier" include Grace Harris of Spokane, Washington; Rev. Grover and Beth Briggs of Shelby, Rev. Brad and Diane Brauer of Malta, and Rev. Emory Robotham of Glasgow—all in Montana. In Minot, North Dakota, I was welcomed by my former colleague, Dr. Jonathan Wagner. In Minnesota, "Land of 10,000 Lakes," I received valuable assistance from Rick Bujanovich, a baker and bear trapper in Becida, near Lake Itaska; De Pickett in Bemidji; Rev. Dick and Nancy Massaro in Grand Rapids; Rev. Robert and Darlene Munneke in Aitkin, who provided an unforgettable evening with only a few hours notice; Harry and Judy Argetsinger near Cambridge; Carroll and Ann Rock in Stillwater; Dorothy Fenton, one of America's most gracious hostesses, in lovely Wabasha; and Marvin and June Wiegrefe in Caledonia. In Minneapolis and St. Paul I enjoyed my tour of Twin Cities Habitat projects, thanks to the kindness of Steve Sydel. In Iowa two families were extraordinarily gracious, Rev. James and Shirley Rozendaal in Guttenberg and Rev. Duane and Orpha Manning in Maquoqueta. In Illinois, three families helped immensely: Rev. Harry and Edna Prince in Kewanee, Don and Pam Kidd in Pontiac, and John and Lori Rodda in Watseka. Edna Prince's suggestion to ship home unnecessary items not only lightened my load but also led to wonderful insights concerning "excess baggage." Two mentors in Indiana deserve particular credit: Doug Taylor in Lafayette and Bob Davenport in Upland. Doug and Cindy hosted me in their home for two nights while I toured Habitat projects in Lafayette. Doug, a veteran cyclist who directed the Lafayette affiliate, introduced me to the nuts and bolts of operating a Habitat organization. In an hour-long conversation, "Coach" Davenport provided an overview on managing a cycling organization while supplying commentary on global politics and philosophy. In Ohio I enjoyed the hospitality of Butch and Sue Crawfis in Bellefontaine and of Joseph Palmer in New Philadelphia.

Various cycling organizations in western Pennsylvania contributed to my maturity in the sport, including the Western Pennsylvania Wheelmen, who offer cycling maps of the region and sponsor rides throughout the year, including annual century rides, of which I completed five. I am also grateful to my colleagues and fellow board members of the National Pike Trail Council, who for a time worked enthusiastically in Washington County to convert railways into trails. Roger Raymond Fischer, triathlete and former member of the Pennsylvania House of Representatives, deserves special recognition for his longtime support of cycling activities in Washington County.

My gratitude extends to several generations of students at Washington and Jefferson College in Washington, Pennsylvania, who loved both recreational and competitive cycling. Dave Curry and Doug Cregan joined me in 1986 for a 432-mile ride across Ohio. Four years later a cycling club was formed at the college, thanks to the initiative of Kyle Rabin and Dave Kuhn. I agreed to serve as advisor. This organization grew rapidly and was quite active in the 1990s. For several years it sponsored a successful competitive cycling team, spearheaded by Jordan Bishko, John Kosar, and Doug Swartz. In 1995, Kosar joined his friend John Hindman in a round-trip ride from Butler, Pennsylvania to Nova Scotia, Canada. Inspired by my trek in 1989, their fundraising ride benefited Habitat for Humanity of Butler County. In ensuing years, the W&J Cycling Association participated in mountain bike races in West Virginia and sponsored a variety of trips, including spring break trips to far-away places such as Big Bend National Park in Texas. Chris Rihn, Ryan Berg, Jason Urchasko, and Brad Wagner provided leadership for many of these initiatives.

Others at Washington and Jefferson College who contributed more directly to this book include Coach John Unice, who took a skeptical approach to my solo cross-country cycling venture by raising the existential question, "why?" Staff members at U. Grant Miller Library were always helpful, particularly reference librarian John Henderson. Dr. Linda Troost of the English Department answered my toughest copyediting questions with accuracy and ease. Debra Trent and Doree Baumgart were attentive, producing copies of my manuscript in a timely and professional manner. I am indebted to the Information and Technology Services Department at the college for essential tech support, including the efforts of Claudia Sweger and Chris Teagarden. Pam Norris, Robert Reid, and Stacy Herrick of the Communications Department were always generous with their time and talent, tackling difficult requests with ease.

Various individuals, including Nat and Grace Roe and Rick and Diana Morris, read early drafts of my manuscript and provided helpful suggestions. Mary Ann Johnson deserves special credit for her invaluable editorial assistance, both in the early stages and again at the end. Christian Amondson, Assistant Managing Editor at Wipf and Stock, responded promptly and helpfully to my every request. I was fortunate to have been in such capable hands. Will Burrows, a former student and gifted artist, created the maps for this book and provided helpful perspective.

Millard Fuller, co-founder of Habitat for Humanity and of Fuller Center for Housing, read an early draft of my manuscript and wrote the foreword. He believed in the story and encouraged me to pursue publication of the manuscript. We corresponded over the years and met in 2005. With his untimely passing in 2009 I lost a friend and the world lost a visionary. I am grateful to the ongoing support of his wife Linda and daughter Faith.

Between 1984 and 2004, cycling became my passion, providing me therapeutic release. Regular rides helped me to regain the physical vitality and emotional equilibrium I had lost through the pressures and sedentary nature of an academic lifestyle. I am profoundly indebted to my family for enabling me to use cycling as a vehicle for growth, physically, emotionally, and spiritually. They supported me through countless training rides and even accompanied me on some of my "outings." Their nurturing presence during the first days of the trek helped me to endure demanding mountainous stages. Through it all, Susan has been my constant companion, offering guidance and support. She read every draft of *The Invisible Mountain* and always provided valuable perspective. I trust her wisdom implicitly and I anticipate her enduring companionship as we climb "the foothills of the Himalayas" together.

1

Openness to Adventure

THE DREAM HAD BECOME a nightmare. Companions—the bicycle, the breeze, sunshine, level terrain, morale—had turned into assailants, tearing, wrenching, beating me down. Even God seemed distant and unavailable. I felt alone, abandoned.

The trek was no spur-of-the-moment idea. For three years I had prepared diligently for the challenges of a cross-country trip. The route was selected, the details honed. Traveling eastward made the most sense. The prevailing winds were more favorable, the ascents more gradual, and most importantly, heading east meant heading home. I was cycling for a noble cause, supported by prayers for a safe and favorable journey. As I left the West Coast I felt confident, like a seasoned surfer riding the crest of a perfect wave.

But now, sixteen days into the trip, my strategy had backfired. I expected harsh winds in the northern plains, but nothing as brutal as continuous gale forces. This was not the wind I knew back East, but a great bursting sweep of wind, uninhibited for hundreds of miles in any direction. For days the wind raged against me, gusting stronger with each passing day. Cycling into a constant headwind was torturous; doing so alone, with no one to block the wind or boost my morale, added to the strain. As the winds intensified, the sealed bearings controlling the pedals deteriorated further. The bicycle was giving out, and each irregular turn of the crank brought it closer to its demise. In this desolate wilderness, harsh elements expose the slightest weakness in man and machine, draining them of vitality.

As I sat by the side of the road, disconsolate, I remembered the question posed by a colleague two months earlier when I told him I would be cycling alone across the country.

"Why, Bob, why?" John Unice asked.

I felt Coach Unice should understand why a forty-five-year-old college chaplain and professor of religious studies at Washington and Jefferson College in Washington, Pennsylvania, was embarking on such a venture. John was the head varsity basketball coach at "W & J," his alma mater. He was committed to physical fitness, and understood the importance of setting personal goals. He knew I was physically prepared. He was aware that I cycled and worked out at the college gym regularly.

John's question demanded deep self-examination. Why would someone want to leave the comfort and security of home and family and embark on a long, perilous journey, alone? That was his point. What did I want to prove?

As I examined my motives and my independent nature, I attributed them to an adventurous upbringing. Having grown up the only child of missionary parents in Costa Rica, a rugged and peaceful country in Central America, I spent my first eight years in a mountainous area of that country, on an orphanage/farm where on a clear day one could see both the Atlantic and the Pacific oceans.

I never regretted growing up in that land of haunting beauty, often called "The Switzerland of the Americas." Bilingualism and biculturalism, inherited gifts, exposed me to diverse perspectives and lifestyles. A byproduct of that upbringing was a healthy curiosity about the world, its people, cultures, and terrain. I longed to become acquainted with that world through travel.

When I was eight years old, my parents moved to the capital city of San José. A highlight of my youth was when my parents purchased a three-speed bicycle on sale at a nearby fire station. It was like new, its lightweight frame and narrow tires promising adventure. Regular commutes to school several miles away, coupled with occasional excursions on weekends, gave me the confidence to go on longer rides. In this mountainous country, I acquired the curiosity to see what was on the other side of the hill.

One day, a short, early morning ride with a friend turned into an unexpected adventure. In search of a real challenge, we headed for the orphanage/farm where I once lived. Taking the highway connecting San José with points north and east, we rode until we came to the base of that hilly road leading to the orphanage, the same road that only twenty years earlier my parents had climbed on horseback.

That ride had always seemed such a long one by car. Now we had come that far by bicycle; only a few miles of hills separated us from our goal. The early morning coolness had dissipated and the heat of the summer day drew perspiration. As we climbed, we stopped at homes for refreshment. In those days cyclists didn't carry water bottles, so common nowadays. At one house, instead of water, we were offered *café tinto*, a thick, syrupy coffee sweetened excessively with brown cane sugar, served piping hot. Somehow, that hot coffee cooled us.

Eventually we came to the farm. It didn't seem possible we had come so far by bicycle. Feeling as though we had climbed to the top of the world, we rewarded ourselves with a cool dip in a mountain stream. There, on that mountain, I celebrated a new discovery. The bicycle, like the horse and the automobile, was an effective means of transportation that could take me most anywhere. That day a bicycle ride became a rite of initiation, a journey into adulthood. A ten-year-old boy came to a mountain and conquered it. I don't remember whether my parents were upset that I was away all day, or whether I even dared tell them where I had been. That day adventure beckoned; the allure of scaling mountains—visible and invisible—had begun.

Ten years later, in college, I shared my sense of adventure with Howard Berry, a close friend, as we dreamed of traveling together around the world. Howard went on to devote his life to the continent of Africa, coordinating relief and service projects as part of his Christian commitment. And when his son was made an honorary member of a Massai warrior tribe, he knew it was he who was being honored.

During my studies at Princeton Theological Seminary, I read about John Goddard, an adventurer who spent his life pursuing 127 goals that he had devised at the age of fifteen. These goals, amazingly varied, included exploring the Nile River; writing a book; composing music; learning to play "Clair de Lune" on the piano; teaching a college course; studying primitive cultures in New Guinea; learning French, Spanish and Arabic; running a five-minute mile; climbing the Matterhorn; circumnavigating the globe; and flying an airplane. I found such an approach to life quite compelling, although I knew I would never be that adventurous.

At that time I purchased a Schwinn Varsity bicycle from a high school student who had discovered that a bicycle pedal could not compete with a car's accelerator. I paid $50 for the ten-speed bike, knowing very little about frame sizes or components.

During the next sixteen years, as I began a career in the pastorate and then as a college professor, the Schwinn saw limited use, primarily on short rides around town with my family or on summer vacations at the shore.[1] By the summer of 1984, in my second teaching position, I was ready once again for adventure. I had recently acquired cross-country skiing and flatwater kayaking skills, but I needed a more expansive outlet.

I dusted off the old Schwinn, oiled its moving parts, pumped up the tires, and began to set goals. Initially, short trips provided adequate exercise, but as my conditioning improved, I looked for greater challenges. Soon I was climbing some of the hills for which western Pennsylvania is famous, and my trips turned into outings.

One day, while looking through a bicycle catalogue, I decided to buy a better bicycle. The Schwinn Varsity was great for kids. It was sturdy and durable, but at forty-two pounds it was too heavy for touring and its twenty-three-inch frame was too small for my lanky six-foot-one-inch body.

At a bicycle outlet in Ohio I selected my first new bicycle, a metallic-blue fifteen-speed touring bike. This time I knew something about frame sizes and components, and I gladly paid $350 for a custom chrome-moly twenty-five-inch Japanese touring bicycle that weighed fifteen pounds less than the old Schwinn. I purchased a roof rack, a good helmet, a pair of gloves, and some cycling apparel.

The thrill of bicycle riding was rekindled and I was ready for some serious riding. Ten- and fifteen-mile-rides turned into twenty- and thirty-mile trips. Cycling was becoming addictive.

The following summer, when I received a grant to participate in a ten-week archaeology seminar in Philadelphia, I spent evenings cycling through Fairmount Park, one of the nation's largest municipal parks. Occasionally I heard a whooshing of air as fifteen or more riders passed me on a club ride, cruising over twenty miles an hour. Once or twice I kept up, observing the use of wind drafting and rapid cadence techniques practiced by racers to maintain high speeds during a four- or five-hour race.

---

1. For a more detailed understanding of this phase of my life, including my transition from the "first naiveté" to the "second naiveté," consult my autobiographical remarks in the appendix.

One day I was at the finish line to see Eric Heiden, the 1984 Winter Olympic gold medalist in speed-skating, win the inaugural US Pro Cycling Championship, the first single-day professional road race in the United States. This 156-mile cycling classic followed a fourteen-mile circuit through the east side of Fairmount Park, including ten trips up the famous "Manayunk Wall," a half-mile hill that starts out steep and then is described as becoming "inhumanly steep." Heiden had cycled during the off-season to keep his legs in shape for ice-skating, and now cycling was paying off in a new career as a member of the 7-Eleven Cycling Team. Attending this event drew me deeper into the demanding world of competitive cycling. I felt compelled to take my bike to the Manayunk Wall and test its rigors for myself.

During the spring of 1986, two college students joined me on a trip across Ohio during "Senior Week," a period between final exams and graduation. We agreed to follow the 310-mile Cardinal Trail across the state, beginning the journey at the western border, near Richmond, Indiana. Four days later we returned home, drenched (it had rained every day of the trip), tired, and sore, but thrilled to have cycled across Ohio and an additional eighty-five miles across western Pennsylvania.

The unending hills encountered during that final section, however, proved painful. Because I was still an inexperienced cyclist, the lack of adequate training and recovery techniques provided costly lessons. The soreness was more serious than I had imagined. By the end of the trip I could barely walk. My knees hurt and the aching calf and thigh muscles limited my mobility, forcing me to climb steps like an invalid.

After that experience, biking became more strategic; building a strong mileage base, by November of that year I had accumulated 2,300 miles. I began regular workouts in the weight room at the college, optimistic about new gains. I felt physically fit, ready for new challenges.

However, lifting weights led to sore muscles, and then pulled muscles. One morning the ordeal peaked when the muscles in my lower back locked. Jolted to my knees by muscle spasms, I crawled back to bed, barely able to move.

A local physical therapist diagnosed a protruding disk and recommended some exercises. One of these, a powerful, relaxing exercise known as "the Cobra," curves the spine inward through a gradual raising of the upper body, alleviating tension and discomfort throughout the back and restoring elasticity to the spine. Sedentary work behind a desk and the passing of years had led to a serious loss of elasticity. But I soon discovered that much of that flexibility could be regained, and then retained, through proper exercising.

Progress came slowly at first, but before long I noticed significant gains. I identified stress-producing situations at work and at home and began avoiding them; when that was not possible, I concentrated on changing my attitude. Discontinuing weight training, I replaced it with more gentle exercises in the swimming pool. Over the winter, while pedaling my bicycle on a stationary wind trainer, I discovered that the rhythmic revolutions of the pedal, coupled with stretching exercises, greatly aided my rehabilitation.

When spring came I was ready to resume outdoor cycling. That July I cycled solo across the mountainous southern tier of Pennsylvania—including some of the steepest series of successive climbs in the United States—crossing New Jersey to the Atlantic shore. That year my mileage exceeded 5,000.

My motivation to cycle across the United States received a strong boost when I encountered a group of cyclists traveling through Washington, Pennsylvania, with attention-getting flags attached to their bicycles. They were part of a larger group of cyclists of all ages trekking across the country on behalf of the American Lung Association. One participant told me that each cyclist had raised $5,000 or more in contributions. The trek had begun in Seattle early in June and was scheduled to arrive in Atlantic City, New Jersey, around the middle of July. The 3,200-mile trip took forty days, and cyclists averaged eighty miles per day. I considered participating in the future, but my teaching schedule made it impossible to leave that early in the summer.

In the fall of 1987 I began cycling year-round, a strategy that led to planning my own bike trek across the United States.

In 1989, after receiving approval for a sabbatical that fall, I initiated plans for a late-summer trip across the North American continent, following a course close to the Canadian border. Bikecentennial, the thirteen-year-old "Bicycle Travel Association" located in Missoula, Montana, advertised an attractive route. Developing an itinerary and locating campgrounds for overnight accommodations, I engaged in a series of progressive weekly workouts that would achieve a base of 2,500 miles by departure time in July.

During the spring semester I informed students, colleagues, and friends of my plans, hoping that some might accompany me. I set July 31 as the departure date; Anacortes, Washington, a small town thirty miles south of Vancouver, British Columbia, became the point of departure. I hoped to arrive in Washington, Pennsylvania by the second week of September, completing the trip of 3,400 miles in a six- to seven-week period. "From Washington to Washington"—the idea sounded catchy.

During the ensuing months eight people indicated an interest in joining me. Pete Katz, the first candidate, walked confidently into my office soon after the announcement went out; I recognized him as W & J's undefeated heavyweight varsity wrestler. He made it clear that he wanted to join me: "I've heard you are biking across the United States this summer, and that's something I've always wanted to do. I would like to go with you from start to finish." He had concluded numerous lengthy bike rides, having cycled with his father to summer vacation spots while the rest of the family went by car.

I welcomed his enthusiasm and his cycling ability, and as I scanned his 240-pound muscular physique I smiled inwardly and thought, "This is great! I'll have a biking companion *and* a bodyguard."

When others indicated an interest in the trip, I invited Dan Grandle, a veteran of six previous cross-country bike trips, to meet with the group and provide motivation. By the time he arrived, the semester was almost over and most students had finalized their summer plans. It had been more than a month since I had talked with Pete Katz. When I called to invite him to the meeting, there was a long pause on the other end. Then I heard him say, apologetically, "I'm sorry, but I don't think I can make it this year. My fraternity brothers have rented a place at the shore and I've gotten a job there that includes a monetary bonus, but only if I stay until the end of the summer."

I told Pete that I understood. How could a long, hot, exhausting bike trip in the company of a religion professor compete with a summer at the shore with fraternity brothers?

The only prospective rider who came to the meeting that night was a student who had injured his knee a few weeks earlier and had undergone arthroscopic surgery. To make matters worse, he had never been on a bike ride longer than fifty miles. I remembered the painful lessons

I had learned during my Ohio trip three years earlier, due to inadequate preparation. His enthusiasm and determination seemed no match for the reality of the situation.

When Dan showed up for the meeting, I invited him to participate in the trip. Having never biked the "northern tier," he expressed an interest in cycling the mountainous western portion of the route with me. Later in the summer, however, with his wife expecting their first child in September and Lamaze classes scheduled for August, he wrote a letter of regret.

One by one all eight prospects dropped out. When I contacted the final rider, a triathlete, early in July for an answer, his reply sounded ominous, "There's no way I'm ready to go; crossing the country is like climbing Mt. Everest." That meant I would be going alone.

I couldn't back out now. Everything had fallen into place: I had reached my base of 2,500 miles, family vacation plans had been arranged so that we could travel together to the state of Washington, and my in-laws had provided their twenty-four-foot motor home for our use. But something was missing. Then a thought struck me—an idea that revolutionized my thinking and galvanized my resolve to cycle solo across the country.

2

A Higher Cause

ONE SATURDAY EVENING, TWO weeks before I left Pennsylvania for the West Coast, I dialed Wayne Armstrong's number. Earlier that morning Wayne, a board member of the newly formed Washington County Habitat for Humanity and a member of our church, had come over to pick up some items left over from our remodeled kitchen. As we carried the sink and counter to Wayne's garage for temporary storage, I asked him to tell me about Habitat.

He explained that Habitat for Humanity is an international, non-profit Christian housing organization committed to abolish poverty housing. Established in 1976 in Americus, Georgia, by Millard Fuller, a lawyer, businessman, and self-made millionaire, its uniqueness consists in establishing a partnership between people who have housing needs and volunteers who can fill those needs.

With funds provided by Habitat and donations of money and building materials, houses are made available for sale to selected applicants. Habitat enables buyers to obtain no-interest loans, which are paid off monthly and through an agreement called "sweat equity," a work program that consists of 500 hours of service.[1]

I learned that Habitat affiliates exist in nearly every state in the United States as well as in over thirty foreign countries. Although 90 percent of all funds raised by the Washington County affiliate stay in the county, 10 percent goes to overseas projects. "A clean, decent home," Wayne said, "can often be built in a third-world country for about one-tenth of the cost here in the States." The more I heard about Habitat the more enthralled I became with its double punch; while 90 percent of the contributions remains in the local area, the remaining 10 percent accomplishes the work

---

1. Each local affiliate determines its own "sweat equity" requirements.

of 90 percent overseas, and then that foreign community tithes 10 percent to another country, and so on. What a recycling vision!

Later that day I reconsidered our conversation. I contemplated the joy my family had experienced designing a new kitchen. I also thought of families, including many in Washington, Pennsylvania, for whom change was frightening, their lives dulled by the lack of opportunity and the absence of wholesome adventure.

The early 1980s had brought hard times to Washington County. A decline in the steel industry led to rampant unemployment, exceeding 15 percent in 1983. The so-called "Mon Valley" at the east of the county was hardest hit. Declining productivity in the steel and coal industries affected virtually every aspect of the county's economy. Young people, disillusioned by the dwindling job prospects, began to look elsewhere for employment.

Wayne Armstrong remembered the 1960s and 1970s as years of abundance, when work was plentiful. As a machinist for twenty years, working ten to twelve hours a day, six and sometimes seven days a week, Wayne kept busy. There was little free time, little time to enjoy the current financial boom. When volunteers were needed for community projects, Wayne didn't respond. His attitude was, "Let someone else do it. I'm too busy." For thirteen years he was too busy even for church.

In 1977 an infirmity changed his life. Some years earlier, in 1960, he was stricken with an unknown muscle disorder that by the late 1970s reached an advanced state, debilitating control and movement of both arms. He was diagnosed with muscular dystrophy and at the age of thirty-eight faced forcible retirement from physical labor. For several years he was despondent, feeling sorry for himself.

Early in 1982, as Wayne listened to a radio appeal for food-drive volunteers, he felt a tug deep inside and discerned in it the whisper of God's voice. He responded to the appeal by agreeing to assist for a short term only, but that whisper turned into a trumpet call and transformed his feeble response into a fervent commitment.

Two years later Wayne left the ranks of the unchurched and joined the Fourth Presbyterian Church of Washington, where my wife Susan served as pastor. Wayne quickly discovered why the church called itself "the Fourth Family," for the church functioned as a single entity, united in its commitment to the surrounding community. As a vital member of that community, Wayne's involvement quickly escalated to legendary status.

He enlarged the church's role in the community even as his own commitment to the needs of that community grew. Through his efforts the church became a center for the government "Surplus Food Distribution" program, and he was designated site coordinator. He served as church liaison with the Greater Washington Ministries (an ecumenical organization designed for community service and outreach) and he was elected to the church's Session (the local church's governing body), where he served as co-chair of the mission committee. He agreed to teach the Senior High Sunday School class and he attended the Lab One and Lab Two seminars, interactive programs designed to enhance "calling and caring" skills, particularly with inactive church members. He also served as a member of the advisory board of Faith in Action, an ecumenical organization that provides assistance to the frail elderly in the community.

In 1988 this man who had been too busy to volunteer for anything received the Washington–Greene County Community Action "Citizen of the Year" award for Washington County. But Wayne didn't seek recognition. "Recognition is like getting paid. What's really important to me," he declared, "is gratitude expressed through a handshake or a hug. That's reward enough."

From inactive citizen to committed public servant, from timid public speaker to outspoken advocate, Wayne became entirely different from the person he was in the 1970s. His former philosophy, "What can I get out of life?" was transformed into "What can I give to others?" His spiritual makeover not only sensitized him to human need, but it also renewed his commitment to family and to God. God became personal, with whom he could relate in profound ways. Having been uncomfortable with situations beyond his immediate control, he began embracing challenges, the bigger the better.

Wayne felt God had given him a desire to focus on "food and shelter." He wasn't clear about the reason, but his church and community involvements clearly bore the mark of that vision.

In the introduction to their book *Everything to Gain*, Jimmy and Rosalyn Carter state that "a third of all American men over the age of fifty-five no longer work!"[2] Although that statistic may no longer hold true, Wayne began to view each retiree as a potential volunteer. He was encouraged by the growth of volunteerism in Washington County during

---

2. (New York: Random House, 1987), xiii.

the 1980s and 1990s. "Many volunteers in our county were unemployed during the early eighties," he said. "Now some are back to work and others are retired, but going through the hard times increased everyone's sensitivity to the needs of others."

People were regularly amazed to learn that Wayne considered his muscular dystrophy as a gift from God, one of the greatest and most profound he had ever received. He certainly agreed with St. Paul's affirmation when he declared: "when I am weak, then I am strong" (2 Corinthians 12:10). Though every human has needs, within each person's incompleteness and inadequacy lies a problem-solving potential. It was this latent potential for partnership that Wayne was able to tap.

Later that evening I telephoned Wayne to tell him about my decision to use the bicycle trip as a fundraiser for the local Habitat affiliate. I volunteered to go "Homeless for Habitat," leaving the comfort and security of my home for six weeks so that at least one additional family might have adequate housing. And I told Wayne I thought we could raise at least $2,000.

He was elated. "I knew all along this trip had great potential as a fundraiser," he said. "I was wondering when you would come around to see it that way."

We laughed together and even shed a tear or two over the prospects. As it turned out, Wayne's excitement prevented him from getting much sleep that night. He had learned never to let an opportunity slip through his fingers, so when he dreamt, he dreamt big. Only that night he dreamed wide-awake.

The next morning, at the eight-thirty worship service, I announced my plans to the congregation, suggesting a figure of $3,400 as a goal, to match the 3,400 miles I would bike. After that service, when Wayne arrived for Sunday School, I told him about my bold revision. His response, however, stopped me in my tracks. "Go back to the $2,000 figure and add a zero," he said. "It won't be worthwhile unless we go for $20,000."

That's what attracted me to Wayne. He had caught the disease known by Habitat volunteers as "infectious habititus," and he lived as though the miracle of the loaves and fishes recurs in the present. I found my own eyes opening to the miracle as well. The bicycle trip had turned into a trek.

Wayne agreed to coordinate all matters pertaining to the trek, serving as publicity chairman, treasurer, and anything else that would be required. By noon of the first day, over $600 had been collected in cash and pledges. One lady placed a $100 bill into Wayne's hands. Each member of Wayne's Senior High Sunday School class pledged $34—a penny per mile—becoming the trek's first "partners."

There was much to do before my departure two weeks later, and I hadn't given Wayne much advance notice. The following morning I met with the Executive Board of Washington County Habitat for Humanity. Wayne introduced me to Gary Nicholls, the gregarious real estate sales-man who was also president of the board, and to Wayne Luther, a Vista volunteer who was helping to organize the chapter by serving as its Executive Director.

As chairman of the trek, Wayne wasted no time in contacting the international Habitat headquarters in Americus, Georgia, providing their staff with information concerning the trek and requesting a list of Habitat affiliates along the planned route. Habitat International responded with enthusiasm, generously placing its resources at our disposal. Telephone calls and letters went out to the affiliates on the list, encouraging them to plan promotional events in connection with my arrival and to solicit lodging during my stay.

While the affiliates responded positively to the request for lodging, certain complications became evident. The route I had selected, although ideal from a cycling standpoint, bypassed major population centers, pre-cisely the areas where Habitat affiliates were located. While some adjust-ments could be made to the route, most of the affiliates on the list still lay beyond my reach. Another problem, more difficult to overcome, involved the lack of lead time sufficient for affiliates to coordinate events around my visit. The month of August seemed impractical for promoting extem-poraneous events, as many families were away on vacation at that time. Nevertheless, despite these problems, we received several encouraging responses.

To help Wayne with the increasing workload, another board mem-ber, Rev. Bob Armstrong, joined the team. A retired United Methodist minister, Bob was eager to use his position within the denomination to help locate contacts and to obtain overnight accommodations on my behalf.

While coordinating the support team, Wayne also embarked upon a publicity campaign, designing T-shirts for me to wear during the trek. The Washington Habitat logo, the words "Washington, PA," and the organization's telephone number were imprinted on the front and back; three deep pockets, adapted to the needs of cyclists, were sewn on the back.

The promotion also included soliciting the media, and soon reporters contacted me, requesting interviews. Gary Nicholls turned one of my training rides into a photo shoot. Wayne contacted Pete Povich, a popular disk jockey and talk-show host in the region, to arrange a half-hour interview on his "Friday Pie-day Show" before my departure.

When Gary presented me with a copy of Millard Fuller's book, *No More Shacks!* I immediately read it from cover to cover. After reading about how Millard, his wife Linda, and several Habitat supporters walked 700 miles from Georgia to Indiana to celebrate Habitat's seventh birthday in 1983, raising $100,000 in the process, I thought, "Habitat's history is full of off-the-wall ideas. My bike trip will fit in rather nicely as a fundraiser." A partnership was in the making.

A few days later the Speakers' Bureau of the Washington County Habitat for Humanity convened and I was invited to provide more details about the trek and to explain my motivation.

I suggested an idea from Paul's first letter to the Corinthians: "In the Scriptures there is an ongoing record of God taking foolish human ideas and blending them into a wonderful mosaic. As the apostle Paul put it: 'God chose what is foolish in the world to shame the wise, God chose what is weak in the world to shame the strong. God chose what is low and despised in the world, even things that are not' (1 Corinthians 1:27–28), to accomplish divine purposes."

A familiar metaphor from Kennedy's 1960 presidential nomination acceptance speech seemed appropriate: "John Fitzgerald Kennedy reminded us not to curse the darkness, but rather to light a candle of hope. The genius of Habitat is that in placing one family in a home, and surrounding that family with support, guidance, and love, a ripple effect begins. Every additional home represents one less crime, one less cry of despair, one more candle of hope."

By now I was sufficiently informed to be favorably impressed with Habitat's holistic gospel. So I continued: "Habitat complements the proclamation of the gospel. The gospel is not good news for the poor and disadvantaged if it is only *preached* to them. The gospel must provide hope for the little guy in society, a hand-up for those who are 'down-and-out.' Our message must be more than words; it needs to be lived out as a lifestyle."

I concluded by disclosing a goal that stretched even Wayne's imagination. "Can we find twenty members in fifty churches in Washington County who will contribute $34 each? That's one thousand people, each contributing a penny per mile. The result would be $34,000." The wineskin of our collective dream stretched to bursting as the idea percolated into the group's collective subconscious. Dividing large goals into bite-size increments would come in handy on those long days in the plains when I cycled over one hundred miles into the wind.

I came from that meeting with the clear impression that these committed people had embraced my plan. The trek had taken on a new meaning; it became an extension of common concerns.

Prior to my departure I attended a dinner meeting of the local Habitat board. The speaker was Jim Tyree, the regional mid-Atlantic director of Habitat International. I attended with the idea that I might have something to contribute, but on this occasion I was the recipient, for I absorbed more about Habitat's vision and strategy in two hours than I might otherwise have learned in months of self-discovery.

The most important lesson I learned was that "the bottom line for Habitat is not building or rehabilitating homes. Rather it is building and rehabilitating lives." Jim emphasized that the most important function within Habitat was the job of the Family Selection committee.

Eventually he addressed the topic of affiliation, an issue that some members of the fledgling board were attempting to expedite. "Don't rush the process," he warned, "and try not to get yourselves caught up in crisis management. It is essential that you spend time together as a board, getting to know one another, enjoying each other as partners and friends." He stressed that enormous responsibilities lay ahead. "Plan for the future; be concerned with the long haul. Habitat is here to stay, and a local affiliate must not collapse for lack of planning, prayer, or training." Then he cautioned, "Select your first family very carefully. It will be under enormous pressure by the media and by outsiders and the future of this Habitat affiliate may well depend upon your initial steps. Measure them carefully, and give the process sufficient time."

I could think of many well-meaning projects within my own experience or memory that had been short-lived or failed due to insufficient planning or overeagerness. As Jim shared words of wisdom with the board, I too, became infected with "habititus."

The following day, on Pete Povich's radio show, I announced four goals for the trek:

- *Adventure* – crossing the North American continent on a bicycle;

- *Spiritual Growth* – becoming less self-sufficient and thereby more genuinely spiritual;

- *Mutual Respect* – sharing goodwill between cyclists and motorists;

- *Habitat for Humanity* – promoting the Habitat concept across the nation.

After months of planning, the order of goals accurately reflected my priorities at that time. Despite my focus on Habitat for Humanity in this chapter, keep in mind that the Habitat connection was a recent goal, even if it was gaining rapidly in importance. Little did I realize at the start of the trip how that fourth goal would transform the other three. A bicycle trip—the challenge of cycling cross-country—was becoming a journey of faith, a vision of cycling for a higher cause.

3

The Ride West

THE JOURNEY WEST BEGAN after church on Sunday, July 23; we had seven and a half days to cross the continent. Susan and our two children, Peter, age twelve, and Sara, nearly eleven, selected the route and sites to visit.

Averaging more than 400 miles a day in the motor home, we still took time to enjoy spectacular sights along the way. Sara's list included Yellowstone, the Badlands, and Mount Rushmore, whereas Peter seemed more interested in grizzly bears, elk, and bald eagle sightings. Susan diplomatically blended all requests into the shortest route possible.

Early on the third day we crossed the Mississippi River near La Crosse, Wisconsin. Later that day, in South Dakota, we gazed at the wide Missouri, its impressive width caused by the backing up of water from Fort Randall Dam, some seventy-five miles downstream. These two rivers would serve a supportive role during my return trip, urging me onward with their powerful currents.

We celebrated the fiftieth anniversary of Badlands National Park with a slow drive through its wonderfully eroded landscapes. Fossils dating back thirty-seven million years had been eroded out of the buttes and gullies in this land that once provided homes and hunting grounds for the Sioux Indians.

In the far southwestern corner of South Dakota, beyond the Badlands, lay the solid granite face of 6,000-foot-high Mount Rushmore, its sixty-foot-high carvings featuring the heads of four famous American presidents: Washington, Jefferson, Lincoln, and Theodore Roosevelt. Although work on the monument had concluded in 1941, the project— including the top of Lincoln's head—had never been completed.

When I asked one of the summer workers at the park about the location of the path leading to the top of the granite peak, I was surprised to learn that no path was available. The mountain, I was told, was federal property, and even touching its face was considered a federal offense. It seems the Sioux Indians were not the only ones to consider these hills as holy ground.

The steepest ascent of our trip occurred west of Sheridan, Wyoming, en route to Yellowstone National Park. The climb involved a dramatic set of switchbacks, up and across Granite Pass, with an elevation of 8,950 feet. As the camper groaned and muscled its way up in lowest gear, I was grateful not to be negotiating these switchbacks on a bicycle. I shouldn't have been surprised, however, when I spotted two cyclists on fully loaded touring bikes riding along the ridge at the top of the pass. There is hardly a road in the United States, perhaps even in the world, where one cannot go on a bicycle.

It felt good to be in high country. The adrenalin flowed as I felt the urge to join this pair cycling through the pristine setting. Later in the day my longing to pedal at high altitudes was indulged as I cycled through Yellowstone National Park, the first and largest of the national parks in the United States. This park, full of natural wonders, is the most extensive thermal area in the world. Its spaciousness, a stronghold for grizzly bear, elk, bighorn, and bison, as well as the bald eagle, great gray owl, trumpeter swan, and raven, also serves the needs of people seeking a refuge from noisy, crowded, and polluted cities. Here parents can show their children one section of wilderness reminiscent of the continent in ages past.

Shortly after entering the park at its east entrance, we crossed Sylvan Pass and stopped for lunch at one of the many small lakes along the south side of the highway. While filling bottles and the camper's tank with fresh water from a mountain stream tumbling towards Yellowstone Lake, I mentally traced its flow eastward along the Yellowstone River to the Missouri, then the Mississippi and finally to the Gulf of Mexico. Each sparkling drop of pure water here at the source of this great watershed symbolized America's bounteous natural and spiritual resources.

While Susan and the children drove ahead to explore the geysers at West Thumb, I pedaled through Yellowstone National Park at an altitude of 8,000 feet, fulfilling a long-standing dream. The lack of previous altitude training made me wonder whether I could perform adequately in the rarified air. But the ride turned out to be invigorating, thanks to the rather gentle terrain along Yellowstone Lake. The bicycle, however, did not fare as well. About ten miles into the ride the pedal crank on the chain side of the bicycle loosened, forcing the chain to wobble. Whenever I upshifted to the highest ring on the triple crank, the wobble forced the chain back to the middle chainring. Careful pedaling and consistent use of lower gears enabled me to reach West Thumb. Tightening the bolt attaching the crank to the bottom bracket worked temporarily, long enough to convince me that the problem had been solved. I concluded that the road vibrations of the bicycle, as it sat on the motor home's bike rack, had caused the crank to loosen. Later on, at a critical point in the trek, the problem would reappear, signaling an impending mechanical breakdown.

We left Yellowstone Park by means of the south entrance, but not before visiting world-famous Old Faithful. The seventeen-mile ride from West Thumb twice took us over the Continental Divide. At Old Faithful, while waiting for the hourly eruption, we were shocked to see how close the huge fires that raged uncontrolled through the park a year earlier had come to the service buildings, only a few yards from the geyser.

Lasting for more than six months, those fires had destroyed 750,000 acres, one-third of the park. Current records show that before 1988 no more than 35,000 acres had burned in any one year, but during 1988, up to 45,000 acres burned *daily*. The unprecedented destruction, caused by a summer-long drought and by unusually high winds that gusted to seventy miles an hour, rendered traditional fire fighting techniques useless. Up to 25,000 people, including military personnel, were needed to fight the fires.

Due to public outcry over the extensive damage, park officials set aside the existing policy of fighting only fires caused by humans. This controversial policy underlies a belief held by many naturalists that significant benefits exist when fires are allowed to burn unimpeded, except when human life, personal property, or endangered species are under threat. The seeds of lodgepole pines, for instance, lie dormant for years on the forest floors, awaiting extreme conditions such as those caused by the intense heat of the fires to germinate. They are part of the renewal that always follows destruction.

In Yellowstone, during the spring of 1989, the waters began leeching from the ashes rich nutrients previously locked in the tissues of trees, enriching mountain meadows and aquatic communities. Grasses replaced the less nutritious sagebrush, providing better grazing for wildlife, now thinned of weaker members.

Yellowstone, born of fire, has long been in partnership with fire, and fire is as essential to its survival as rain is to a rain forest. The fires of Yellowstone have taught us, if nothing else, to trust nature and to learn from its lessons.

Our stay in Yellowstone was brief, but towards dusk we saw moose gathering in the meadows and along the streams running parallel to the highway. Watching these stately creatures feed gracefully is a nightly routine for guests at the park. We felt fortunate to observe this splendid event. Further south the changing colors of the setting sun over the Tetons brought a fascinating day to a majestic climax. We arrived at a campsite close to the Idaho border well after dark.

Our route the following day, the sixth of the trip, paralleled the old Oregon Trail, so significant in the development of the Pacific Northwest a century and a half earlier. That evening's brilliant sunset, viewed from our campsite at Baker, Oregon, was magnified by widespread smoke drifting northeast across the Blue Mountains, caused by forest fires burning throughout the state.

I pondered the meaning of that unusual sight, how smoke from destructive fires actually heightened the splendor of the sunset. Events we designate as harmful—misfortune, disaster, tragedy, illness—need not be viewed as inherently evil. Nature reveals that adversity, including setbacks and delays, are essential to existence, often transforming the quality of life and even enhancing it in positive ways. Theologians remind us that tragic events in our lives are penultimate and not final. Tragedy, though a valuable part of life, need not have the final word. It provides perspective and can create a dynamic of determination that serves as a pointer to the future and to that which is ultimate.

The next day, as we rode along the Columbia River, a bend in the road brought us to an unforgettable spectacle. Before us stood the 11,230-foot snow-capped peak appropriately named Mount Hood, towering in majestic singularity. For miles motorists are rewarded with unobstructed views of this stunning sight.

That afternoon we crossed the mouth of the Columbia River at Astoria, Oregon. Before us lay the Pacific Ocean, not far from the camp where the explorers Lewis and Clark wintered after reaching their goal on November 8, 1805. It had taken us only seven days to travel 3,000 miles, while their expedition of 4,000 miles had taken more than thirteen months, not counting a winter's rest in North Dakota.

My trek, a solo trip across the northern tier of the continent, would have been impossible in those early years. Aside from the difficult terrain, the unpredictable inhabitants, and the lack of roads, the ownership of much of this unchartered Northwest was still disputed in 1805. I was glad to be traveling in the modern era, for any problems I encountered would surely pale next to theirs.

While a solo trip across that region was practically unthinkable in the period of Lewis and Clark, to do so on a bicycle would have been impossible. Research into the history of the bicycle reveals that the first two-wheeled machine didn't come into existence until 1818, when the *draisienne*, a clumsy machine propelled by paddling one's feet against the ground, was first exhibited in Paris.[1] In 1839, a Scottish blacksmith named Kilpatrick Macmillan invented the first self-propelled bicycle, marking 1989 as the bicycle's sesquicentennial. My transcontinental trek turned out to be an anniversary celebration.

In 1861 the Michaux family of Paris invented the first usable bicycle, with pedals attached directly to the large front wheel. But this model, dubbed "Boneshaker," was neither safe nor comfortable, and it weighed over 150 pounds. The first relatively lightweight bicycle was made by James Starley, of Coventry, England, who by the 1870s had reduced its weight to fifty pounds, including a track-racing version that tipped the scales at twenty-one pounds.

The development of the modern bicycle required additional modifications to Starley's prototype, including the invention of the pneumatic tire by John Dunlop in 1888, the development of the diamond-pattern frame by 1893, and the introduction of sealed gears inside the rear hub by H. Sturmey and J. Archer around the turn of the century.

In the United States, on the heels of such advances, cycling became both popular and fashionable. Cyclists organized into clubs and soon competition developed between local groups. Intrepid individuals began to test their courage and skills with long-distance rides, including crossing the North American continent. One solo rider, Tom Winder, cycled the perimeter of the country in 274 days, covering some 21,000 miles.

1. Information on the evolution of the modern bicycle is taken from the article "Bicycle," by Alan H. Gayfer, *Encyclopaedia Britannica*, Macropedia, Vol. II, 15th ed. (Chicago: The University of Chicago, 1974), 981f.

In 1895 George T. Loher, a butcher from Oakland, California, and member of the Acme Cycling Club, was one of the first to cross the United States by a difficult northern route, over some of the wildest and roughest portions of the country. This remarkable journey was made on a Stearns Yellow Fellow wheel, a diamond frame bicycle that came equipped with only one fixed gear and no brakes. The newly formed American Dunlop Tire Company provided the pneumatic tires. Loher's ride, like mine, was completed alone.

The roads he used out West were barely passable on a bicycle. Often they consisted of a sand or clay base, strewn with rocks for traction and deeply rutted. Layers of dust or mud added to the challenge. At times the route required that he ride the ties along railroad tracks, surely a hazardous venture.

It was only Loher's ingenuity, and that of blacksmiths along the route, which allowed him to complete his journey. An unsuspected threat came from mischievous children who entertained themselves by poking pins into his balloon tires. His eighty-day trip required the replacement of numerous tires, a front wheel, handlebars, and the front forks. He concluded the journey successfully by writing in his journal: ". . . if you ever cross the continent on a bicycle, I sincerely hope you will meet with better roads, more congenial people, and last but not least, a stronger bicycle than I had."[2]

A century later, I pedaled with far greater confidence.

Leaving the Lewis and Clark campsite and the details of their memorable expedition behind, we found a campsite on Long Beach, the longest beach in the state of Washington. There Peter and Sara joined me for a tentative dip in the frigid, weed-strewn waters of the Pacific Ocean. No one was in sight, so we assumed we had the entire beach to ourselves. Suddenly Susan yelled a warning as the hard wet sand became a raceway for jeeps, passenger cars, and other road vehicles, all darting about on the sandy freeway. The wind and the pounding surf had kept us oblivious to any sounds but our own.

Later that evening I enjoyed my final training ride. I headed toward the town of Ocean Park, arriving at dusk. To the west I saw a rise in the

2. George T. Loher, *The Wonderful Ride* (San Francisco: Harper and Row, 1978), 144. Ellen Smith, Loher's granddaughter, published the journal with commentary.

road, leading past the dunes. Biking up the hill, I observed that the beach below was filled with people. The beach scene seemed surreal, like looking at a still frame, for no one moved or spoke. Considering the possibility that an accident had occurred, it took me a few moments to process the situation. Then I realized I was witnessing a nightly ritual on the Pacific, for beyond the waters a majestic sun set slowly in the horizon. The poetic phrase, "from sea to shining sea" came alive on that occasion, for the sea literally *was* shining. Each day of the trip west the words from *America the Beautiful* were taking on new meaning.

The following afternoon we enjoyed a breathtaking view of Puget Sound and its surrounding mountain ranges from the top of Seattle's Space Needle. The Olympic Mountains lay to the west, and on the east, extending the full length of Washington and Oregon and well into California, stretched the Cascade Range, highlighted by the 14,410-foot Mt. Rainier. The day was overcast, limiting our visibility; even Mt. Rainier was hidden from view. But thirty miles to the north, separating the United States from Canada, were the emerald green San Juan Islands, and close by, near the town of Anacortes, was the ferry landing where my return trip to Pennsylvania would begin early the next day.

Anacortes! That name had been in my mind and on my lips for many months, whenever I explained my proposed cross-country route to those who inquired. The unusual name derived, not from an explorer's, as one might think, but from the name Anna Curtis, the wife of an early settler.

We camped that night at Washington Park, next to Puget Sound, and enjoyed a hike along the rugged coastline until dusk. As I watched ferries plying the currents in the distance, bridging the outlying islands with the mainland of two nations and facilitating a vast international network, my thoughts turned to my own human network: to the people in "Little" Washington, Pennsylvania (as the city is known, to distinguish it from Washington, DC); to "The Fourth Family"; to Wayne, Gary, Bob, and others of the Washington County Habitat for Humanity team; to Millard Fuller and his incredible vision to eliminate poverty housing; and to those who would benefit from this fundraiser.

I was part of a team headed by one who had said, two thousand years earlier, "Truly, I say to you, as you did it to one of the least of these my brethren, you did it to me" (Matthew 25:40). There is no limit to what one individual can do, when he or she is part of that team. Together we were heading home, captured by a vision, empowered by a dream.

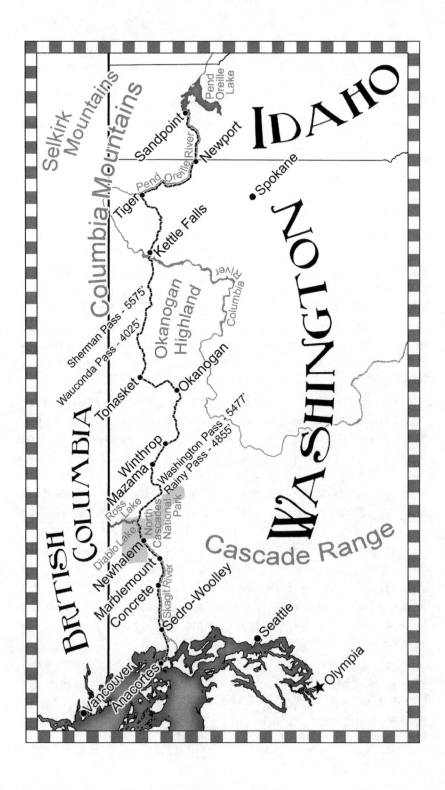

4

Mountains: The Physical Watershed

STAGES 1-6: STATE OF WASHINGTON— ANACORTES TO SANDPOINT, IDAHO [458 MILES]

Stage 1 (July 31): Anacortes to Marblemount – 75 miles

THE AIR WAS HEAVY with the texture of departure. Though gray and overcast, the sky showed promise. With the temperature in the mid-fifties, it was a propitious day to begin cycling across America.

I adjusted my helmet and checked the tire pressure; it was below the maximum of 110 pounds, but adequate. The Bikecentennial map was clearly visible in its plastic pocket atop the handlebar bag. A small pack on the rear rack and my handlebar bag were all I needed for the day. Most of my gear, including a lightweight tent and sleeping bag, was still in the motor home.

I quickly ran through the inventory of essential items: tools, spare inner tube and patches, tire pump, raingear, sunglasses, gloves, cyclo-computer, water bottles, fruit, sandwiches, energy bars, Fig Newtons, and some spending money.

Shortly after nine o'clock I turned my back to the Pacific Ocean and headed toward the rising sun. At the ferry landing I waved goodbye to Susan and the children. We had agreed to meet that night at a camp-ground seventy-five miles away, a pattern that would repeat itself until we crossed the Continental Divide at Glacier National Park in Montana. After that I would be on my own.

The trek began privately, without fanfare. Wayne Armstrong had hoped for a rousing sendoff by local Habitat volunteers, but a scheduling error and the remoteness of Anacortes from the two affiliates in Seattle and at Linden, on the Canadian border, made that impractical.

The first day's ride looked relatively easy, on paper. A short detour would take me to Route 20, my course for five days to the Idaho border. But the first nine miles were more challenging than I had anticipated. The recommended route took me along Marine Drive, away from the main road, and then on additional back roads before joining Route 20. The Bikecentennial maps, which I intended to follow faithfully, were designed to help cyclists avoid busy highways and congested areas. But the first stretch of road made me question the wisdom of such a detour, at least for my purposes. The road was quite hilly and narrow, and not as well paved as the main highway.

When I arrived at the town of Sedro Woolley, I decided to follow the recommended route once again, this time a twenty-five-mile ride along South Skagit Highway, a route parallel to Route 20, but along the other side of the Skagit River. Although the route was scenic and practically deserted, the road had recently been tarred and chipped, and was far too bumpy for my highly pressurized tires. I felt like I was riding the old "Boneshaker" instead of my comfortable touring bicycle. That "highway" left me sore, frustrated, and exhausted. Rejoining Route 20 at the town of Concrete, I decided to avoid further detours while riding through the state of Washington. I could see no reason to suffer needless pain and aggravation on side roads when Route 20 was well paved and had adequate shoulders.

The rest of the day involved a gradual climb along the broad Skagit River, with a cool ocean breeze to my back. I marveled at the greenish-yellow water of the Skagit, an unusual color created by the glaciers at the river's source.

That afternoon, during one of my breaks, as I thought about Susan and the kids, I glanced down the highway and noticed the familiar Yellowstone motor home, which we call "the Little House," pulling over behind me. This was the first of numerous impromptu encounters.

Later in the day, as I neared the campground we had selected for our first night's stay, the motor home approached once again, this time from the opposite direction.

"We have to go back to Marblemount," Susan called as the vehicle came to a stop. "The campground ahead is practically abandoned, and there is nothing for the children to do."

Although I resisted the idea of backtracking several hilly miles to Clark's Skagit River Resort, I knew that watching me pedal was not Peter and Sara's idea of entertainment. Going back proved to be a wise decision.

There were two unusual features about our campground. The first was the numerous rabbits that ran about, the offspring of domesticated rabbits set free some years earlier. The pets and their abundant offspring had chosen to remain in the lush green meadows around the campground instead of risking the dangers of predators in the mountains. One drawback to this veritable Garden of Eden quickly became evident when we decided to play a game of badminton on the lawn. It was hard to concentrate on the birdie while avoiding the ubiquitous rabbit droppings.

The other unusual feature of the resort was the very small chapel that had been transported to the current site. A popular venue for weddings, the chapel seated about a dozen people. The notion of a small chapel awaiting me at the close of the first day of cycling across America seemed appropriate, considering that my last name, Vande Kappelle, means "of the chapel" in Dutch.

That night I fell asleep immediately. The day's seventy-five mile ride, my second longest of the year to date, had been a gradual but steady climb. The bone-jarring journey along the South Skagit highway, combined with eight days of driving the motor home cross-country, had taken its toll.

Stage 2 (August 1): Marblemount to Winthrop – 94 miles

The second day of cycling proved to be one of the most awe-inspiring days of the entire trek. Marblemount, at the edge of the North Cascade National Park, is known as "The Entrance to the American Alps." This gleaming landscape, sculptured by the Ice Age, lived up to its billing, for the fifty-eight-mile climb that morning to the summit at Washington Pass included breathtaking vistas at every turn of the road.

The cool crisp mountain air made the seventeen-mile ride to Newhalem quite pleasant. This tidy little town, which provides housing for the hydroelectric plants of the Skagit River and its tributaries, was once the object of regular sightseeing tours. At the turn of the century, James D. Ross, superintendent of the Seattle utility, administered the construction of gardens as well as dams in this area. In a small canyon near Newhalem the utility's employees grew imported herbs and introduced foreign birds and animals to create an exotic setting. Sightseers from Seattle came regularly by bus to see the garden and the nearby dams. Illuminated paths and ponds, accompanied by music from outdoor loudspeakers, added to the nighttime spectacle.

While these amenities no longer exist, a trip through North Cascade National Park's natural setting is still one of America's most impressive natural wonders. The park's setting includes more than three hundred glaciers, hundreds of jagged peaks, blue alpine lakes, and clear streams. This area, home to a host of wild birds and animals, provides anglers with outstanding trout fishing.

From an economic perspective, the foremost wealth of the Cascades lies in its hydroelectric plants. Between Newhalem and Ross Lake, a distance of fourteen miles, are three impressive dams, owned and operated by Seattle City Light.

Beyond Newhalem the climb intensified as the road wound between majestic peaks and through tunnels. A sudden drop after Diablo Dam led to a renewed steep ascent around the southern tip of Diablo Lake and up to Ross Dam.

Between Ross Dam and Rainy Pass, the first major summit of the trek, a distance of twenty-three miles, I found myself stopping every few miles to quiet the pounding of my heart and to relieve the buildup of lactic acid in my calves. Although I had previously crossed the steeper Allegheny Mountains in southern Pennsylvania, those mountains included climbs of only several miles before summits were reached. Today's ascent consisted of fifty-eight miles of sustained climbing. My legs and lungs had never undergone such non-stop demands. Stops at scenic overlooks, real and imagined, helped relieve my fatigue.

A note in the Bikecentennial maps reminded me that until 1972, Ross Dam had been the end of the line for eastbound traffic. The area connecting the Skagit and Columbia drainages was so precipitous that it had required one hundred years of lobbying by settlers and industries on the eastern slopes before the state legislature agreed to build a highway.

With eight miles to go before reaching Rainy Pass, I was struggling mightily. At one rest stop I noticed another cyclist coming up the mountain behind me, progressing rhythmically in staccato-like fashion. With head bent low and arms extended outward in front of his crouched frame, he was resting comfortably on aero handlebars. A recent invention, these handlebar extensions, with optional armrests, attach directly to drop handlebars, extending the rider's aerodynamic tuck while adding comfort to long distance rides. Having recently been used at the 1989 Tour de France road race, they enabled cyclist Greg LeMond to overcome great odds at the closing time trial and win the Tour by eight seconds.

Waving the rider over, I learned that he was training for a national road race in New York State later that summer. He had won several such races before and was taking time off from work to train in these demanding mountains. He was rapidly building to a distance of 150 to 200 miles a day. When he displayed an interest in my companionship, I decided to follow him, knowing that I needed the motivation of a strong cyclist to help me reach Rainy Pass. Because my gearing was lower than his I climbed with less effort, and for several miles I actually led *him* toward Rainy Pass.

What a difference a strong cycling companion makes, mentally and physically. Teamwork and good pacing techniques lessened the tedium of the climb and helped reduce the painful feeling in my muscles and knees. Without any additional breaks, we quickly reached Rainy Pass. A sign indicated that we were crossing the Pacific Crest National Scenic Trail, a popular hiking trail that stretches 2,400 miles from the Canadian border to Mexico.

Beyond Rainy Pass, the highway continued its climb for five additional miles before reaching Washington Pass, at an elevation of 5,477 feet. Greg continued his ride and I proceeded to the overlook, where the Little House awaited me. On that rocky, wind-swept mountaintop, I gazed in amazement at Liberty Bell Mountain, its two bookend-like peaks supporting a low hanging rock mass. The jagged, razor-sharp cluster was imposing, with snow patches adding a touch of color to the dull-gray silhouette. I studied the highway as it coiled its way down the mountain. Like a downhill skier, I examined my line of attack, thrilled by the precipitous descent.

The ride to Washington Pass and the view from the overlook were magnificent, with one potential rival ahead, namely "Going-to-the-Sun" highway, the famous ascent to Logan Pass in Glacier National Park. Like an explorer charting a course, I set my sights for that spot on the Continental Divide, still 600 miles away.

When I crossed Washington Pass, I experienced a phenomenon that recurred on ensuing summits: the tailwind nudging me up the mountain shifted suddenly into a headwind. Acting as a brake on the sharp descents, it also brought with it cold rain, which stung like ice pellets as I darted through turns and dashed around gorges at speeds up to forty miles an hour.

As I cycled through the mountains of Washington, the temperatures ranged comfortably in the fifties and sixties, but whenever I descended, the temperature dropped dramatically. With wind chills below freezing, I quickly learned the necessity of donning a bicycle jacket and tights. On those descents when I didn't wear tights, my legs shook from the cold and became practically useless. The bicycle maps had forewarned me, "CAUTION: Be prepared for sudden, drenching showers, accompanied by cool winds. These can be dangerously chilling."

The eighteen-mile descent from Washington Pass was exhilarating, like an endlessly plummeting roller coaster ride. But the excitement of the moment was tempered by sudden changes in road conditions, momentary lapses of concentration, and the paralyzing effects of the wind and cold against my skin. These steep descents require extreme concentration, for reaction time is greatly reduced.

Having heard of wipeouts and severe injuries under similar conditions, I wrapped my fingers tightly around the handlebar drops. Feathering the brakes while tucking my upper body into the most aerodynamic position possible, I barely peeked above the narrow slit between the tops of my glasses and the rim of the helmet.

Oh, the joy of a long descent after a sustained climb! It is unmatched by any other feeling, and is the greatest reward of a cross-country bicycle trip.

The thrill of conquering the first major summit along the North Cascade highway and the excitement of that long downhill descent were quickly subdued by the thirteen-mile-ride from Mazama to Winthrop. On that day this scenic ride along the Methow River was accompanied by a strong headwind, the first of many I encountered on my journey. What should have taken forty-five minutes became a tedious struggle lasting twice that long.

At Winthrop I caught up with Greg, the racer. He, too, had "hit the wall" along the Methow River. Winthrop, a carefully restored western gold-mining town, proved to be an excellent place to rest my weary bones. After ninety-four miles of riding, I needed to get "out of the saddle." Despite the challenges of the mountains, I was surprised to find myself less exhausted than the previous day. Still sore all over, I nonetheless felt a reservoir of energy.

That night I telephoned Wayne. I had agreed to call him every other night, and he had consented to be home between nine and eleven o'clock, Eastern Time. That procedure provided supporters in Washington County with regular updates and kept Wayne informed of my safety.

To facilitate the process, Washington County Habitat for Humanity had supplied me with a "calling card." What a useful tool this piece of plastic turned out to be! A plan of emergency was worked out in case Susan or I were unable to meet at predetermined locations. Susan also received a card, with Wayne's home telephone and other numbers available around the clock.

Wayne kept a log of all our telephone conversations. His entry for that night reveals that I called at eleven o'clock (eight o'clock Pacific Time). Then he recorded these words, "Bob said he was calling tonight from a campground where he had just used the *ladies'* shower." Well, that was partly true.

I had planned on taking a shower right after making the call. The telephone was outside the bathroom, on the wall between the entrance to the ladies' and men's shower. A hard rain was falling, so under cover of an umbrella I had rushed around the corner of the building and through the first door, which I thought to be the men's shower. It was unoccupied, so I placed my clothes and toiletries on the counter and returned to make the telephone call. Only later did I discover how close I had come to a major embarrassment, for as I spoke on the phone, women began occupying the room. At the conclusion of the call I sheepishly asked a lady to retrieve my personal items from *her* shower room. Her puzzled look spoke volumes.

Stage 3 (August 2): Winthrop to Tonasket – 69 miles

When I arose on the third morning of the trek, the temperature was forty-two degrees—quite frigid for August 2, even in the mountains. The decision to leave Anacortes prior to August 1 had been a wise one, for snow would soon be flying across these mountains. This day proved to be my fastest day of cycling in the state of Washington, with an average speed of sixteen miles an hour. A slow, steady climb of ten miles led me over Loup Loup Pass, followed by a cold and rainy descent of nineteen miles into the town of Okanogan. A personal rain cloud seemed to follow me.

The terrain on the eastern slopes of the North Cascades is arid, much different from the moisture-rich western slopes. Mount Baker, the most prominent peak on the west slope, receives an average of over one hundred inches of precipitation annually, whereas Okanogan, one hundred miles to the east, receives only a desert-like twelve inches.

As I rode into Okanogan that morning, an attendant at a quick-stop service station, dressed in jeans, remarked that this was the first day all summer he had worn anything other than shorts. Knowing that the place averages ninety to one hundred degrees daily during the summer, with hardly any rain, I felt odd riding into town with the temperature in the low sixties and with rain falling. Despite the rain, sprinkler systems were operating in every orchard.

I arrived at Tonasket early in the afternoon, refreshed by a wind-aided ride. Tailwind rides are always blissful. If they arrive at the end of a day's journey, even if only for a few miles, they can atone for a long, discouraging day. As I waited for the motor home, I was surprised to see Greg, my traveling companion of the previous day. He was embarking on another lengthy ride before calling it quits for the day. This was the last time I would see him.

Stage 4 (August 3): Tonasket to Kettle Falls – 85 miles

The fourth day's ride, like the second, involved two demanding climbs; the final one took me across Sherman Pass, the highest summit thus far at 5,575 feet. As I neared Sherman Pass, I heard the whining and droning of chain saws as loggers felled timber from the 22,000 acres destroyed by fire during the previous summer.

Today's ride produced several frustrations. The dull pain I previously felt in my knees and legs now became excruciating, preventing me from standing up to pedal for more than a second or two at a time. I dismounted every twenty or thirty minutes to stretch my leg muscles, attempting to alleviate the needling pain.

Despite the 2,000-mile base achieved prior to the start of the trip, the pain indicated inadequate preparation. I had ignored the guidelines for increasing mileage gradually. The first week's ride of 575 miles, much of it in the mountains, more than doubled the highest weekly total I had accumulated that year. The guidelines suggest that a weekly total not exceed 10 percent of the previous total. Now I was paying with pain for this sudden jump in mileage and intensity. My stamina, however, was there, and I was pleased with the climbing ability I had gained throughout the week.

The other frustration came from detours and delays caused by road repairs. Climbing towards Wauconda Pass, I came across seven miles of impassable roadwork. By coincidence, the Little House had passed me earlier and was waiting at the construction site. For a moment I struggled with my stubbornness and pride, believing that the goal of biking across the continent couldn't be reached unless every mile was cycled. But common sense prevailed as I carried the bike into the camper, reluctantly accepting a ride across the broken roadway. It was foolish to compromise my safety or that of the bicycle by trying to pedal across unsafe terrain.

An amusing event occurred as I neared my destination for the day. At the town of Kettle Falls, where the highway crosses the Columbia River, I was unclear as to the location of the campground my family had chosen. Stopping at a grocery store to ask directions, I was astonished to hear the clerk say, "Are you Bob?" Then she explained herself. "I have a note here from Susan." In it were directions to the campground several miles away, across the river.

When Susan had entered the store several hours earlier and explained the situation, the clerk had offered her paper and pen. But when Susan explained her intention to post the note along the highway, the lady responded, dejectedly, "Oh, then you won't need me."

Susan quickly replied, "Oh, yes, my husband will need you. Sometimes he misses visible signs, so he always checks with people along the way for directions."

Susan knew that I favored verbal over visual communication, so she commented to the children, "I hope dad is himself when he comes to this spot." Fortunately, I was.

Susan had selected a campsite along the Columbia River, in an attractive National Parks Campground. I couldn't resist an invigorating swim in the *cold* water. Peter and Sara had gone swimming before my arrival, so they remained at the shore, relishing my pained expression and wisely refusing to join me.

That night Wayne had good news. An endorsement letter for the trek had arrived from Millard Fuller, founder of Habitat, which Wayne would forward for my use with Habitat groups along the route. He also informed me that Byron Smialek, a columnist for the local Washington, Pennsylvania newspaper, had agreed to carry updates on the trek in his widely read column. In addition, Wayne had received permission from two local malls to post displays of an enlarged map of the United States, on which my route had been marked in red. Every few days Wayne would mark the route with a small flag, indicating my progress. Pledge cards also accompanied the displays. The trek would not fail for lack of publicity.

Stage 5 (August 4): Kettle Falls to Newport – 100 miles

Friday's ride proved to be my first "century ride" (a trip of one hundred miles or more) of the year. On this, the fifth day of the trek, and the fifth day of climbing, I found myself adjusting to the physical demands, paying less attention to my aches and pains and more attention to my surroundings. It was the first sunny day of the trip, around eighty degrees, and ideal for cycling. The scenery along the Little Pend Oreille River and past the numerous alpine lakes was peaceful and relaxing. A sharp drop brought me out of my reverie and into the town of Tiger. My water bottles were practically empty and I always welcomed towns as the source of replenishment. But I soon discovered that downtown Tiger consisted of three buildings, only one of which looked promising.

When I knocked on the door, a voice inside yelled, "It's open!" As I entered I saw three people inside the one-room building, all annoyed at the interruption. It looked like an office, for the boss, an assistant, and a secretary were seated behind separate desks.

"Sorry to bother you," I began, speaking as politely as possible. "Could I fill my water bottles?"

There was a pause before the boss replied, curtly, "We don't have any water."

For a moment I stood in disbelief, unwilling to take "No" for an answer. My eyes glanced hurriedly across the room. When I saw a refrigerator in one corner, I thought about offering to pay for some refreshment, but as my eyes refocused on the boss it didn't take a genius to see that the conversation was over. I had no choice but to leave.

Putting myself in his shoes, I could understand his attitude. Given the location, it was likely that cyclists knocked at the door all summer, requesting water. An opportunity seems to exist for some enterprising ten-year-old to profit handsomely by selling cold lemonade somewhere along that route in downtown Tiger.

As I walked out the door I felt a bit desperate, for I was miles from nowhere, with only a few sips of water left in my bottle. As I headed toward my bicycle I saw two female cyclists sitting by the roadside, making peanut butter sandwiches. I decided to join them, hoping for some water. They had come from New York City and were in the process of relocating to the state of Washington. At that moment, as they pedaled across the country, a moving van was transporting their belongings to their new home. One of the riders was a college teacher, and the other, from Brazil, was her pupil. They had cycled only part of the way, having taken the train across North Dakota and portions of Montana. When I inquired about the winds in the plains, they remembered mostly favorable winds through Montana. That was not good news for me, since I was moving in the opposite direction. They also warned of voracious mosquitoes in eastern Montana. Their tidings were not altogether pessimistic, however, for they did recall seeing a campground a half hour's ride away, where they were sure I could fill up with drinking water.

The fifty-mile-ride from Tiger to Newport passed through one of the most sparsely populated regions of the state. Since traffic was light, I decided to stay on Route 20, dismissing the map's suggestion to cycle on the other side of the Pend Oreille River. I couldn't forget the jolting ride along the Skagit River four days earlier. Staying on the main highway gave me a better chance to arrive at Newport by five o'clock, when I was scheduled to meet Susan. She would transport me to Spokane that evening for dinner with Grace Harris, founding president of Spokane Habitat for Humanity.

About eight miles past Tiger I spotted a campground, the Blueslide Resort. "The best in the west," the manager said when I questioned him about the quality of the water. "The minerals alone will keep you alive." Later on, whenever I filled up with lukewarm water from taps along the way, I remembered that cool refreshing water and imagined myself drinking "the best in the west."

Continuing toward Newport, I heard the sudden blast of a horn behind me. A glance in the rear view mirror revealed a logging truck, loaded sky-high and barreling rapidly towards me. Since no other vehicles were in sight, I wasn't overly concerned. Loggers are generally quite friendly, as long as you stay out of their way. In the past they always gave me a wide berth. I didn't realize this driver had a different intention until I heard the deafening roar closing in and felt the familiar turbulence caused when tractor-trailers pass at close range. I was riding the white line, but "Mr.

King-of-the-Road" felt I belonged on the other side of the shoulder, or better yet, off the road altogether. Here, on this otherwise deserted highway, he missed me by no more than a few inches.

My immediate reaction was to yell at the trucker. My next reaction was to yell even louder. Long after he disappeared, I still felt angry. What right did he have to endanger human life, especially *my* life, by using his truck as a weapon? I came close to the boiling point, rehearsing the tongue-lashing I would give him if he cared to come back and discuss his behavior rationally. But I'm sure he had no interest in rational discourse; I didn't either.

Did the fact that it was Friday afternoon—payday—have anything to do with this provocation? I could remember at least three other close calls back in Pennsylvania, all on Fridays, each caused by reckless or inebriated drivers. Questions entered my mind in rapid succession. Was there an adequate explanation for this trucker's attitude? Was he being playful, or was he just hostile to cyclists? If hostile, was it caused by the recklessness of a previous cyclist? Perhaps he was just an angry person, bored by his circumstances, picking on the "little guy." I wondered if his anger was directed at my participation in what many in the United States consider a "leisure" sport for the wealthy.[1]

After working out my frustrations, I finally began to calm down. It was time to work on my own attitude, my own anger, because one of the goals of the trek involved increasing good will and respect between cyclists and motorists. So why allow anger as my traveling companion? I steered the bicycle well on to the road's shoulder, concentrating on riding defensively. My task wasn't to change other people's behavior, but to control my own. I still had a long way to go.

Stage 6 (August 5): Newport to Sandpoint – 35 miles

I arrived in Newport, near the Idaho border, a few minutes before five o'clock. There was just enough time to ride the extra mile to complete a century before my scheduled rendezvous with Susan. But upon reaching the junction of Route 20 and US Route 2, where we had agreed to meet, I saw no indication of Susan or the Little House. Susan had been in Spokane that day, so I figured that the motor home was caught in Friday

---

1. Oddly enough, in most countries outside the Northern Hemisphere, it is just the opposite; the bicycle is a means of transportation for the poor.

afternoon rush-hour traffic. I waited calmly for half an hour, performing routine stretching exercises to unwind. After forty-five minutes I considered calling Wayne, but I paced the sidewalk instead, not wanting to alarm him. I rode to the edge of town and then stopped at a gas station to perform some minor adjustments on the bicycle. Finally the motor home arrived, almost two hours late.

Susan explained that the battery had gone dead. Without her knowledge, the alternator belt had broken earlier that morning and she had traveled eighty miles and even stopped for gas as the battery lost its charge. To compound the problem, the indicator light on the dash was not working, so Susan was oblivious to the impending breakdown. Fortunately, the battery had gone dead while the motor home was parked at a center for recreation vehicles in Spokane.

Susan had notified Wayne of her plight, following the emergency plan we had devised. By not following that procedure, I had subjected myself to needless anxiety. "When in doubt, read the directions." Nowadays, people wouldn't consider taking a trip such as mine without using cell phones, but in 1989 cellular communication was in its infancy.

We had agreed to meet Grace Harris at Whitworth College, on the outskirts of Spokane, for a picnic supper. Fortunately, this gracious lady was not alarmed at our late arrival and we shared an enjoyable picnic on the college's chapel patio. We remained on the campus until dark, discussing the history and remarkable accomplishments of Spokane's Habitat affiliate, begun in the spring of the previous year. In just over a year the volunteers had completed one new house construction and rehabilitated two older homes, including a five-bedroom house built in conjunction with the Neighborhood Centers' Homeless Project, to serve as transitional housing for several families at a time.

Grace, the petite and energetic president of Spokane Habitat, informed me that though she was a retiree, she hadn't retired from serving others. Through her example I was reminded that service organizations such as Habitat provide remarkable outlets for retirees and help keep the spirit of volunteerism alive across America. What a model older folks can provide for younger generations! I applaud all Grace Harrises and those who emulate them, young and old alike.

With improving health and longer life spans, people in the "second half" of their lives have greater opportunities than ever before for involvement in the life of their communities. As former president and Mrs.

Carter affirm, quoting a speaker at a national conference for retirees: "The talents, wisdom and energy of our retirees are badly needed by our communities . . . and retirees who are active and involved have a new sense of self-worth, a source of daily enrichment. The aging process is slowed."[2] Grace Harris is testimony to that.

From Mrs. Harris I collected whatever information I could to send to the as yet unaffiliated Washington County Habitat for Humanity. As a college teacher, I was interested to learn that Whitworth College students had begun a Habitat chapter on campus, which works closely with the Spokane affiliate.

The next morning I made it a point to stop at a well-stocked bicycle shop. My bicycle had taken a good deal of pounding in the mountains. The pedals and toe straps had worn out, and I needed a new pair of gloves. The bike's headset was checked for wear. It would be a long time before I would have access to a shop like this, perhaps not until Minneapolis. This was the time for preventive maintenance.

Later in the day the Little House transported me back to Newport, and from there it was an easy thirty-five-mile ride to Sandpoint, Idaho, with its beautiful setting on Lake Pend Oreille. The campground, connected to the town by a scenic bike path, was located across the lake, several miles south of town.

From the campground I telephoned Rev. George Tolman, interim minister of Central Christian Church in Kalispell, Montana. Both he and Bob Lehman, a retired Presbyterian Christian Education Director, were committed to Habitat, and they mentioned they were planning a reception in my honor two days hence. That visit constituted my first in-depth encounter with a Habitat organization, and I was expecting a memorable visit.

2. *Everything to Gain*, 95.

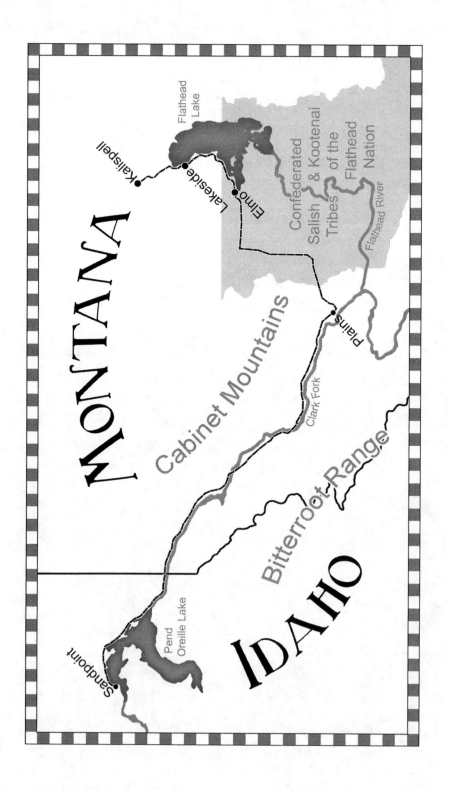

5

Flathead Valley

STAGES 7–8: IDAHO AND WESTERN MONTANA—
SANDPOINT TO KALISPELL [204 MILES]

Stage 7 (August 6): Sandpoint to Plains – 118 miles

I LEFT THE CAMPGROUND by eight-thirty Sunday morning and re-crossed Lake Pend Oreille, passing quietly through the slumbering town of Sandpoint, Idaho. I had a long ride planned for the day, heading southeast along Route 200 to my destination in Plains, Montana, 118 miles away.

I pedaled briskly several miles out of town when suddenly, while negotiating a curve, I heard pieces of metal strike the road behind me. At that same moment I began to lose control of the bicycle. Something was clearly wrong with my bike, but what? Had my frame broken? Would I be able to continue the trip? In that split second, a thousand thoughts raced through my mind. As I fought to gain control of the bicycle, I had a sinking sensation, as if the bike were collapsing. That split second seemed like an eternity.

Following that momentary lapse, my instincts immediately took over. I brought the bicycle under control, grateful that no cars were around. I secured the bicycle and began to assess the damage. The bolt connecting the seat to its post had snapped in half, causing the seat to give way. The pieces of metal I had heard falling on the pavement were the sleeves used to adjust the angle of the seat.

It was a minor accident, but without a seat I couldn't go very far. Retracing my route, I was able to recover all the missing pieces. Now all I needed was a bolt. But where could one find a bolt for a Japanese bicycle at nine o'clock on a Sunday morning, in northern Idaho?

I looked around and found myself alone. The few houses across the street looked vacant. Then I noticed a bicycle parked in front of a bungalow behind one of the houses. Surely someone with a bicycle would be sympathetic to my plight. Even a temporary repair would suffice.

I walked to the door and knocked, but there was no answer. I knocked a second time, and waited. Finally someone stirred inside, and a young lady came to the door, dressed in her nightgown. After apologizing for the disturbance I asked, awkwardly, "Is your husband home?" She nodded, after hearing my explanation, and re-entered the house, closing the door behind her. Only later did I realize the startling implications of my question.

A while later, although it seemed much longer, she reappeared, this time with a bucket of bolts. "See if these will help," she said. She explained that she and her husband were moving, and that they had stayed up late to finish packing. "I don't know why this bucket of bolts wasn't packed. The rest of my husband's hardware has been sent on."

At that moment, without looking into the bucket, I knew one of those bolts would fit. A familiar biblical passage came to mind, "I will never leave you nor forsake you." Later, as I examined that passage, I found a more suitable translation in the Revised Standard Version: "I will never *fail* you nor forsake you" (Hebrews 13:5). I was counting on God to be my navigator, but now I could say God was also my mechanic. What began as a disaster ended as a blessing. After a short delay, I was on my way.

I pedaled into Montana feeling elated, for two states were behind me, with only eight to go. But my euphoria quickly subsided when I envisioned Montana, traversed by the Rocky Mountains. Montana, the fourth largest state in the nation, was also the longest state I would cross. North Dakota was a distant 800 miles away.

For the remainder of the day I rode along the scenic Clark Fork River, against its northwesterly flow. To my right stood the majestic Bitterroot Range, separating Idaho from Montana, and on the left, the equally splendid Cabinet Mountains. The river's current, slowed by dams, spread out into broad reservoirs. At times, when the road hugged the side of the cliff, I stared in amazement at the mountains towering around me, rising abruptly from the water's edge. I felt as though I had been transported to a distant Norwegian fjord. My euphoria returned.

As the day wore on, my elation receded yet again. The wind was bothersome, and the temperature soared over the one hundred-degree mark. By the end of the trek I would remember this as the hottest day of the journey.

Suppertime came and went, and still two hours of pedaling remained before I could join my family for a home-cooked meal. I was hot, tired, and parched. To make matters worse, the condition of the road surface deteriorated twenty-six miles from Plains. Traffic was light, so I ranged across the road searching for a smoother line for my narrow, highly inflated tires.

Caught in this exasperating ebb tide, I overtook two cyclists standing by the roadside, looking intently at a map. They were from Hawaii, cycling coast to coast. At this point they were disoriented, unable to find the campground they had planned to use that night. I was pleased when they accepted an invitation to join me in the final push to Plains. A strong pace and teamwork enabled us to finish strongly. I marveled at the timing, at this rhythm underlying life, for in that moment of exhaustion on my part and confusion on theirs, our meager reserves were boosted by timely companionship.

It was almost nine o'clock when we rolled into Plains, following my longest day of biking ever. Like a ping-pong ball, my emotions had alternated all day, up one moment, down the other. But I had reached my destination, and that was gratifying.

Stage 8 (August 7): Plains to Kalispell – 86 miles

The next morning I headed for Kalispell shortly before eight a.m. My hosts had arranged a television interview at three o'clock in Lakeside, a small community on Flathead Lake, fourteen miles south of Kalispell. Lakeside was seventy miles away, and I didn't want to be late. Since my companions from the night before were enjoying a leisurely start and had no deadlines to meet, I pushed off alone.

I knew it would be a tough day as soon as I felt the wind coming from the northwest, for today's ride would take me in a northerly direction. Less than a mile out of Plains the challenge was compounded by a five-mile ascent. Fortunately the wind was light and the twisting climb up the hills provided shelter. The night's rest had rejuvenated me, and I felt strong as I climbed.

The terrain at the top consisted of heavily forested rolling hills. I was entering the first Indian reservation of the trip, an area allocated to the Confederated Tribes of the Flathead (primarily Salish, Kalispel, and Kootenai). In the distance my eye caught a small moving dot. Realizing it was another cyclist, I became absorbed in an animated chase to catch up.

My new companion, a broker from Chicago, was currently on vacation, cycling to Billings. Two years earlier he and a friend had pedaled from Chicago to Denver, and now, as he relived those memories, he was creating new ones.

We cycled together for thirty-five miles. When the terrain changed from forested hills to open range, we began working as a team, pacing one another in an attempt to lessen the effects of the wind, increasing our speed and productivity. At one point, however, we slowed to a quiet halt, attracted by a family of foxes traveling along the deserted road. They stood motionless, some eight paces away, ears perked, smelling our scent. We played a waiting game, man and beast, facing one another with intensity and curiosity. Finally, having less time than they, I turned to leave, taking with me a treasured memory.

Tom and I rode side by side, talking. When I told him the purpose of my trip he responded, without breaking cadence, "You can count me in." I wasn't quite sure what he meant until I realized I had been sharing my strategy to locate volunteers who would pledge $34 towards the trek. That was a real encouragement, having a fellow cyclist believe so readily in my cause. Tom became my first non-Pennsylvanian "partner."

We parted company at Elmo, a town on Flathead Lake; it was the first town we had seen since Plains, forty-seven miles away. I continued ahead, impatient to reach Lakeside. It had become quite hot by now, and I hoped to arrive early enough to cool off in the lake before the television interview.

A short distance beyond Elmo I saw a disconcerting sign: "Road Work Ahead." Having been warned about repairs along this stretch of the road, I had the impression I could pedal through them. But that turned out to be impossible. A group of workers informed me that the flagman up ahead had orders to prevent cyclists from passing through on their own.

My only choice was to catch a ride in a passing pickup. When none stopped, I decided to take greater initiative. At the barricade I approached the driver of an enclosed pickup and explained my predicament. At first he seemed reluctant to take me across the eight-mile construction zone, but eventually he relented. I lifted the bicycle into the pickup truck cap and climbed next to it, sitting on the wheelwell.

As soon as the flagman waved us on, I realized this was the worst roadway I had ever seen. The base consisted of shifting sand and loose rock. Huge earthmoving and grading machines darted about, filling the air with dust. As we picked up speed, stones began to fly. Bouncing off the truck's undercarriage, they created a "rock music" all their own. The pickup swayed from side to side, struggling to gain traction on the loose surface. I crouched down in my cramped quarters, trying to see out the window. The floor of the pickup and the base of my seat became cold from the wet sand slapping against the undercarriage. Up ahead a water truck was spraying the sand and gravel, trying to keep down the dust.

At one point another vehicle passed us, sending stones into our windshield. This infuriated my driver, who cursed loudly and began to pursue the perpetrator, driving as if he were drunk. We careened down the road at a reckless rate of speed, with no guardrail to protect us from the sheer drop on our right. It brought me no comfort to see a six-pack of beer on the seat next to the driver.

When we finally came to the paved section, I expected the pickup to slow down, but that didn't happen. A horrible thought crossed my mind. What if this man refused to stop? What would I do? A few minutes later, an even more perverse idea crossed my mind: what if I were being abducted? I panicked when I examined the tailgate and noticed that the handle was missing. There was no way for me to escape my enclosed cell.

The driver eventually pulled over at a scenic overlook. While he had been looking for a safe place to stop, I had been imagining the worst. After helping me get out, he offered me a drink of soda. I accepted it gratefully, disguising my mixed emotions.

I reached Kalispell, the Flathead County seat, around five p.m., having enjoyed a refreshing swim at Flathead Lake following my television interview at Lakeside. The informal roadside interview had gone surprisingly well, and I was eager to watch the result on the evening news at Bob Lehman's house.

As I passed the courthouse I noticed people milling about, as though waiting for someone. One man casually took a picture as I rode by. I continued into the heart of Kalispell, the largest city in northwestern Montana, paying little attention to the occurrence, until a van pulled up next to me and a woman called out, "Are you Bob Vande Kappelle?" (Was this the lady from Kettle Falls, I wondered, or was my wife up to one of her tricks?) I nodded, surprised to be a celebrity in Kalispell, as she continued, apologetically, "Can you come back to the courthouse? We have a reception for you."

At the courthouse I saw a large "Welcome to Kalispell" banner, with my name, correctly spelled, held up by members of the local Habitat organization, Flathead Valley Partners, all looking rather chagrined. They had been told to look for a cyclist wearing a blue helmet with a white stripe down the middle, but as I rode by, facing them, all they could see was a mostly white helmet. They also had the mistaken impression that I knew to stop at the courthouse. The miscues translated into an uncertain welcome. The man who had taken the picture as I whizzed by the first time was just practicing for the moment when "the real cross-country cyclist" showed up. We laughed at our confusion.

While showering at the Lehman's house, I heard a shout from the living room, "You're on, Bob!" My interview was being broadcast on the evening news and I was preoccupied. I quickly dried off and rushed out, partly dressed, in time to catch a glimpse of myself riding down the road. Missing my television debut was a high price to pay for cleanliness.

The news team had expanded my interview to include a special segment on poverty housing. As George Tolman explained later, "Your visit on behalf of Habitat is *news* in Kalispell." Fortunately I caught an abbreviated version of the interview on the eleven o'clock news.

The Lehmans used my visit as an opportunity to host a western "potluck" get-together, attended by friends and members of Habitat's Steering Committee. Hospitality is important out west, and easily expressed. Dinner that night was a real family affair as children and adults mingled, laughing, sharing, and conversing. Flathead Valley Partners was on the verge of incorporation, and its members were enthusiastic. Two months later this organization became the first official Habitat for Humanity affiliate in the state of Montana. These jubilant, committed folks were a source of great encouragement as I geared up for the next stretch of the trek: cycling solo across Montana, North Dakota, and Minnesota to the Mississippi River, over 1,250 miles away.

That night over $200 was received towards the trek, with $1,500 pledged toward Flathead Valley Partners. A significant share came from Bob and Carolyn Lehman, our gracious hosts, who attributed a recent windfall to my arrival.

The following morning I placed my bicycle in George Tolman's station wagon and we returned to Kalispell. This was no joy ride, as I soon discovered. Our first stop was a radio station, followed by another. After a third interview, this time with a newspaper reporter, George took me to his office, where we discussed his friendship with Linda and Millard Fuller, whom he had met some years earlier in Zaire, Africa. George had caught "infectious habititus" from them, and now he was doing his best to contaminate others. He had previously founded Habitat groups in Tucson, Arizona, and in Orange County, California. Later, following his successful stay in Kalispell, he went to New Mexico to help organize a Habitat affiliate there. Rev. George Tolman was a modern visionary, one link in a long chain of witnesses to God's power and love.

Although he served in an interim capacity, Reverend Tolman, a retired minister from Arizona, was anything but a stop-gapper. This go-getter accomplished more in one year as an interim than some might accomplish full-time in ten. As I pondered his secret, I felt it was his style, so fluid and disarming, that made him so special. His was a rare quality, combining Yankee ingenuity, southern charm, and western attire.

Following a tour of Flathead Valley's substantial Food Bank, we joined the "Over the Hill" group at a popular café for the daily mid-morning break. This group consisted of a dozen or more professionals from the Kalispell area who met to exchange pleasantries, discuss projects, and plan outings to the nearby Glacier National Park and the surrounding Rockies. After our informal meeting, the members participated in what looked like a harmless game. I was almost lured into playing, until I learned that the winner paid the bill. I never saw people more anxious to *lose* a game.

In Kalispell I learned a great deal about the surrounding Flathead Valley. A guidebook describes the area with a rhetorical question: "What other spot in the United States is bordered by the majesty and serenity of three spectacular wilderness areas and the nation's premiere system of wild and scenic rivers?"

Lying on the western slope of the Continental Divide, in the midst of the Rocky Mountains, the Flathead area is a nature lover's paradise. The territory includes portions of Glacier National Park, Flathead National Forest, parts of Flathead Lake (the largest natural freshwater lake west of the Mississippi River), and three wilderness areas, totaling 1.3 million acres of land suited for backpacking, hunting, fishing, and sightseeing. It also includes the Bob Marshall Wilderness, which extends sixty miles along the Continental Divide. Here visitors can view the wildlife as well as scenery such as the Chinese Wall, a fifteen-mile-long spectacular Cambrian limestone reef with a one-thousand-foot vertical face. Fossils of extinct animals up to one billion years old are found embedded in its limestone.

Flathead Lake offers a variety of water sports and fine fishing. This lake holds the Montana record for lake trout, having produced a fish that measured forty-one and one-half inches in length and weighed forty-one and one-half pounds.

Despite this region's natural bounty, there is distressing poverty among Flathead's inhabitants. One of the Habitat partners expressed the dilemma this way: "The expression 'you can't eat scenery' typifies the struggle of those who have chosen to live in this area of natural splendor but then go broke trying to make a living." Even here, in "paradise," there is a vital need for organizations such as Habitat.

6

Going-to-the-Sun

STAGES 9–10: WESTERN MONTANA—
KALISPELL TO GLACIER NATIONAL PARK [93 MILES]

Stage 9 (August 8): Kalispell to Glacier National Park – 53 miles

I CYCLED OUT OF Kalispell accompanied by Christine, a young lady of Filipino and Puerto Rican ancestry, who borrowed a bicycle and took time from work to extend further the Kalispell spirit. She explained how difficult it was to find approval for bicycle riding among the impoverished families with whom she works. Those who are poor often disapprove exercise of this nature.

I saw this bias as a variation to the "cycling is a leisure sport for the wealthy" syndrome that I had pondered during my encounter with the logging truck on the way to Newport, Washington. I wondered if cycling for fitness or competitive cycling could be promoted in poverty-level communities, particularly as a way to elevate the self-image of its youth and to help families overcome the endemic hopelessness and sense of despair.

As we rode along a back road, I discerned the outline of the mighty Rockies to my right. My heart beat faster in anticipation of the thrill that awaited me. In less than twenty-four hours I would be cycling up the world famous "Going-to-the-Sun" highway to Logan Pass, the highest and most spectacular point of the trek.

After Christine's departure I continued to Columbia Falls, a town located at the northern tip of Flathead Valley, near Glacier Park's western entrance. While there I visited the Renfrews, active participants in Flathead's Habitat. A tour of their cabinet shop, which receives orders from many of the western states, convinced me that stalwart folk like the Renfrews are the real "heartbeat of America." It could be argued that this wonderland's true bounty is its caring citizens.

It was a perfect day to cycle into Glacier National Park, an area so stunning in beauty it is called the "Crown of the Continent." The sun was warm, but neither too hot nor too bright. I was optimistic about tomorrow's weather, hoping it would be equally favorable. That was the day I was "going-to-the-sun," over the Continental Divide.

Today's ride was a relatively easy fifty-three miles. My objective was to cycle as far into the park as Avalanche campground, only sixteen miles from Logan Pass. I had been warned to get an early start up the summit, since the western half of the highway, from Lake McDonald to Logan Pass, was closed to cyclists from eleven a.m. until four p.m., due to the increase in traffic during that period and the narrowness of the road.

I arrived at West Glacier around three o'clock, crossing the railroad that would be my constant companion across Montana and North Dakota. The "Northern Tier" bicycle route was becoming increasingly attractive to cyclists precisely because of its proximity to the Amtrak passenger trains that ride this Burlington Northern Santa Fe (previously Great Northern) Railway. If a person wants to cycle only a portion of the route, or if an emergency arises requiring the cyclist to abandon the trip, an Amtrak station is generally nearby.

At four o'clock, when the road along McDonald Lake reopened to bicycles, I left West Glacier and continued to Lake McDonald Lodge, a hotel originally built in 1913 as a private hunting lodge. Parked in front were several bright red 1936 White tour buses, their canvas tops rolled back to provide unobstructed views of the park's scenery. I felt transported back in time and space to a magical Shangri-la. A walk through the lodge's paneled lobby and across the grounds to the lakeside convinced me that Susan and I should return to this place someday.

The five-mile ride to Avalanche took me along the turbulent McDonald River, its onrushing waters reverberating in my ears. As I pedaled to the music, I felt a strong urge to continue, past the campground, onward, upward, toward Logan Pass. The conditions were ideal for the ascent, and I felt quite confident that I could reach the pass before dark. But as I approached the campground, I curbed my enthusiasm. The climb would have to wait, for I had promised to spend the evening with my family. The Little House and its occupants would soon depart for Pennsylvania without me, and I would be on my own for the remainder of the trek.

After supper we went for a stroll along a creek, enjoying the view from the platformed walkway called the Trail of the Cedars. Susan and Sara felt adventurous and decided to hike the two-mile Avalanche Lake Trail. From the lake they were able to view numerous waterfalls cascading down 2,000-foot-high rock walls. Hoping to experience a special moment with my son at a critical pre-teen stage in his life, I joined Peter as he explored Avalanche Creek, a stream filled with potholes scoured by stones in the swift-flowing water that plummeted from Sperry Glacier.

Peter and I performed gymnastic feats on fallen logs bridging the stream and then decided to walk upstream to the first falls. There we found a place along a protruding ledge and sat down, surrounded by the roar of the cascading water and the spray that sent dancing crystals high into the air. Something about that spot, its altitude, solitude, and the rarified mountain air, encouraged us to disclose our innermost thoughts. We talked about values and about growing up, the topics of conversation a father yearns to have with his son at a pivotal point in their relationship. In a few hours we would be apart, and Susan needed Peter's strength and support during my absence.

Stage 10 (August 9): Glacier National Park to St. Mary – 31 miles

I tried not to awaken the others as I prepared for the day's climb. It was five-thirty and still dark. I remembered the warnings: "The road to Logan Pass is closed to bicyclists every day from eleven in the morning until four in the afternoon. That means you must start early in order to cross the pass, even if you're a strong cyclist." I heard that park rangers patrolled the road around ten-thirty, picking up any stragglers not likely to make the summit by eleven o'clock. So I awakened early, not wanting to suffer that indignity.

The distance to the top was only about sixteen miles, but it involved a vertical climb of 3,500 feet, to an elevation of 6,664 feet. On the previous day a park ranger had told me that this ride was considered the tenth hardest bicycle climb *in the world*. That certainly couldn't be true, but it made me panic.

To make matters worse, I awoke that morning to the sound of rain, not the hard pounding of a thunderstorm, but rather the misty rain so common in the Pacific Northwest. I slipped into tights and a cycling jacket, making sure the rain poncho was in my pack in case the weather changed for the worse.

The ride along McDonald Creek was not particularly steep at first, but as the valley narrowed, the grade steepened. I cycled alone for seven miles until I reached a tunnel, and there, sheltered from the rain, I stopped to talk with a group of cyclists from Vermont. Having been transported to that spot by a van, they were about to begin their ascent. These were not road-hardened cyclists, but tourists out for some fun. After a few minutes of conversation I continued ahead, alone. This day's ride had been in my thoughts for months. I was climbing one of the world's outstanding scenic routes. I wanted to be alone, one-on-one with the mountain.

"The Curve," beyond the tunnel, marked the beginning of the true climb, for here the road swings abruptly away from the creek and begins to hug the rock wall. From that spot to the top is about seven miles, and six of those miles are along a cliff face known as the Garden Wall, with an ever-deepening drop-off on the right side. Behind and below were mountain lakes, pines, and snowfields. Above, as far as I could see, were mountain peaks, dabbed with splotches of white.

It is here, along the Garden Wall, that the glories of "Going-to-the-Sun" are revealed. I could see the road almost all the way to the top. Engrossed in the mountain's misty moodiness, my senses became riveted to the lakes, waterfalls, glaciers, and high cliffs that unfolded before my eyes. Yes, Glacier National Park "was meant to be felt, not idly viewed."[1]

I thought about the Indians, the original inhabitants of this rugged, beautiful land. For 10,000 years they had lived here. Then about 200 years ago the Blackfeet, a people of legendary ferocity, displaced the ancient Kootenai. In 1890, when a copper strike was announced, the Blackfeet received $1.5 million for their lands, living since on a reservation to the east of Glacier National Park.

The names of many landmarks in Glacier come from Blackfeet legends, the most famous being the story of Going-to-the-Sun Mountain:

> "Long ago great adversity visited the Blackfeet. Gone was their glory in war, gone their skill and strength; famine held them. Troubled by the distress of his favorite people, the Great Spirit

1. Udall, Stewart L., and the editors of "Country Beautiful," *The National Parks of America: Centennial Edition* (Waukesha, Wisconsin: Country Beautiful Corporation, 1972), 57.

sent among them a warrior of fine mien, a chief who knew all things, to instruct them in the way they should live. Again they became a great people, regaining their dominance over all tribes. As quickly as he had come, the chief departed up the lofty slopes of a mountain to the west, and as he went, amid lightning and thunder, clouds of snow eddied about him. After the storm the sun blazed forth, and the Blackfeet saw that the snow on the mountain formed the profile of the great chief as he was going to the sun."[2]

Around eight-thirty the drizzle turned to rain and my visibility was lost to the thick clouds that rolled in. Being able to see only a few feet in any direction, I became more concerned with the traffic. The road was narrow, and only a low wall protected me from the chasm to my right. Beyond that six-inch-high wall there was nothing to break a fall, nothing for thousands of feet. The highway, completed in 1933, had been designed and built during Model-T days, hence its narrowness.

Soon the grade steepened, bringing with it a change in surroundings. The rock wall gave way to a green hillside, and the road changed direction. Suddenly a sign appeared, "Summit, Logan Pass," and just ahead was the visitors' center. I was stunned to reach the Continental Divide so quickly. It wasn't even nine o'clock, and I had reached the top. After the ascents in the North Cascades, I had expected a greater challenge in the Rockies. The sudden arrival was a letdown.

Of course the climb would have been more difficult and time-consuming had I carried fully loaded panniers up the mountain. Soon I would be carrying that extra weight, but the road was all downhill to Pennsylvania, wasn't it?

Looking for warmth and shelter, I pushed the bicycle under an overhang at the visitors' center and entered the lobby. Because of the unpredictable weather, capable of providing snow at any time of the year, rangers always kept a fire burning in the fireplace. I sat down by the hearth, removed my wet shoes and outer clothing, and turned the fire irons into makeshift hangers. Before long other cyclists joined me in front of the fire.

As I looked out the windows, I could see nothing but fog. Occasionally, however, gusts of wind swept the fog away, providing glimpses of staggering peaks, menacing, chill, and ghostly, surrounding the pass.

2. Federal Writers' Project, *Montana: A State Guide Book* (New York: Hastings House, 1949), 386.

Shortly after ten o'clock Susan and the children arrived, disappointed by the ride up the mountain. The thick fog had enclosed the mountain completely as they ascended, totally obscuring their view.

During a pause in the rain we went outdoors, determined to see something of this wild grandeur. We had heard of Glacier's trail system, consisting of more than a thousand miles of trails, the most extensive of all the national parks. But before we had hiked one hundred yards, the wind whipped up and the temperature began to drop rapidly. The ranger informed us that a major storm was moving in, with no letup expected. We raced to the motor home as a raging wind swept walls of rain toward us, striking the camper in pelting sheets. We were glad to be together in the warmth and safety of the Little House, but dismayed by the mountain's elusiveness.

By noon the weather had deteriorated to the point where cycling down the steep eastern slope was out of the question. As the parking lot became covered by the torrent, I was forced to accept a ride, this time *down* the mountain.

Several miles later, however, the weather changed dramatically. The fog lifted, the sun came out, and we stared in awe as we emerged into a world of crags, towering upwards for thousands of feet.

Since this was our last day together, we decided to continue north into Canada. We crossed the border at Chief Mountain, finding ourselves in Waterton Lakes National Park, Canada's smaller but no less spectacular version of Glacier Park. In Canada, I resumed my cycling, thereby adding an international dimension to the trek. I returned along Chief Mountain International Road and pedaled until I reached the border.

I was surprised at the simplicity of crossing through customs on a bicycle. The officer on duty asked just three questions: "How long have you been in Canada?" to which I replied, "Less than an hour."

"Did you purchase anything while you were in Canada?" The answer was obvious, since I hadn't seen a store or even met a Canadian citizen during my brief visit.

The questioning ended with, "Do you have any alcohol or cigarettes to declare?" We both laughed as I responded, "I think there are several six-packs hiding here somewhere," and I was waved through customs. Unfortunately, since the events of 9/11, even simple border crossings have become arduous affairs.

As I crossed the border, the contrasting terrain caught my attention. To my right the imposing Rockies protruded ever skyward, while to my left stretched the deeply undulating wilderness known as the Great Plains.

That night we camped on the Blackfeet Indian Reservation, along the Lower Saint Mary Lake at the base of the Rockies. I could have remained in this paradise for days. But I had been-to-the-sun. It was time to push on, into the open plains "east of Eden." Ahead lay the land of Nod,[3] a vast, unprotected, wind-swept expanse.

The trek was shifting to a more intense phase. The physical mountains were behind; invisible mountains lay ahead.

3. Nod means "wandering" in Hebrew. On the origin of this and the preceding biblical metaphor, see Genesis 4:16.

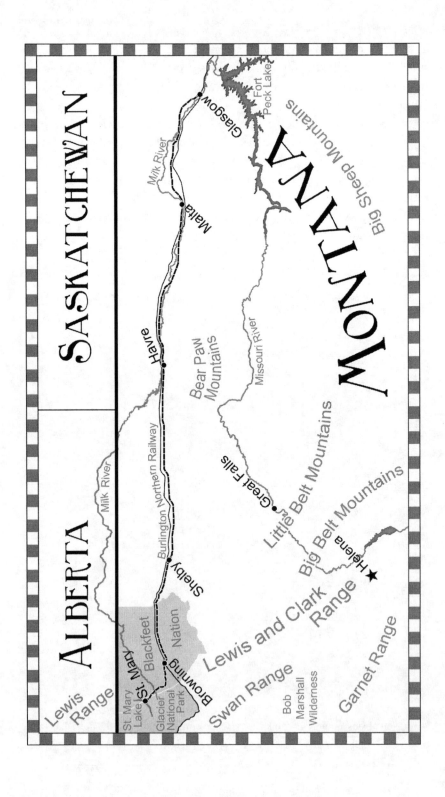

7

East of Eden

STAGES 11–15: CENTRAL AND EASTERN MONTANA—
ST. MARY TO GLASGOW [366 MILES]

Stage 11 (August 10): St. Mary to Shelby – 96 miles

EACH MORNING INVOLVED A departure, but today's departure was the most difficult. After ten days of steady support, the time had come to say goodbye to my family and to leave the Little House, my home away from home. Susan had to return to her work, after first visiting her brother and his family in Colorado. The children were road weary and eager to see their only cousins.

The encouragement I had received from my family had helped immensely as I crossed the mountains. Our daily encounters, whether on the road or at the end of the day, had been uplifting. I would miss the hugs, smiles, and words of cheer of those who loved me unconditionally.

That morning I went outdoors by myself, for that seemed like the best way to deal with my convoluted emotions. Susan, caught in the same emotional riptide, remained inside the camper, giving me space to prepare for the solitude ahead.

I checked the bicycle with greater care than usual, tightening the pedal cranks one last time. Mechanically, the bicycle had functioned well since Sandpoint, but I didn't want to take any chances. I intended to travel as lightly as possible, but not to overlook anything essential. Before leaving, I handed the bottom-bracket toolset to Susan. I didn't want to carry heavy items unnecessarily. I assumed there would be bicycle repair shops along the way, should I need parts or a specialized tool. "You're sure you won't need the tools?" Susan asked, as a final word of caution. "No," I assured her, "I'll be fine."

I loaded the tent, sleeping bag, groundcloth, and self-inflating mattress on the bicycle rack and secured them with shock cords. The three water bottles—red, white, and blue—were in their cages. I had everything I needed for normal roadside repairs, including inner tubes, extra spokes, and a spare tire.

Pushing aside the empty feeling within, we bid our farewells. I left first. A few miles later I heard a horn honk and arms waved as the Little House went by for the last time. My destination was Shelby, ninety-six distant miles away.

Beyond the town of St. Mary the road began a steep ascent and I followed it, higher and higher, gaining some two thousand feet in altitude before leveling off. I hadn't expected such a climb. I had deviated from the Bikecentennial route, which proceeded through a remote area of Canada, in order to trim a day or two from the length of the trip. Without the benefit of my topographical maps, I had inadvertently chosen the more demanding route. During the climb I also encountered a stiff crosswind coming from the Continental Divide, making more difficult my adjustment to the newly acquired thirty-five-pound load. But there was a trade-off; the peaks along the Continental Divide shone proudly in the brilliant sun, and the slow climb gave me plenty of time to enjoy the view.

At Cut Bank Creek I turned left and followed a back road into Browning. At this point the strong wind turned into a tailwind, and it pushed me along that deserted stretch of road at the brisk speed of twenty-five miles an hour. I sped past Indian villages, but each looked deserted. Where were the adults? Where were the children? No one was in sight.

At Browning I stopped to visit the Museum of the Plains Indian, located in the heart of the Blackfeet Reservation. The museum featured the work of Native American Indians, including paintings and traditional crafts. Adjacent to the museum was a wigwam, the setting for an authentic display of native customs by members of the Blackfeet Nation. As I signed the guest register at the museum, I saw a familiar name above my own. My family had preceded me by a few hours.

I ate lunch in the shade of the trees close to the museum's entrance. A youthful member of the Jehovah's Witnesses used the opportunity to provide me with literature and to shed some light on my spiritual condition. In return, I familiarized him with Habitat's vision, hoping to enlarge his horizon. There was something amusing in this role reversal, as an eighteen-year-old adolescent, dressed in a suit, proselytized a college religion professor dressed in cyclewear.

After lunch the wind intensified, and from the way it was blowing, I knew I was in for a treat. Gusting to forty miles per hour, the tailwind blew me down the highway at an astonishing rate. With seemingly little effort I pedaled a loaded bicycle at thirty miles an hour, arriving in Cut Bank before three o'clock. As I stood at a fruit stand, a downpour struck the area, blown by a wind so strong that when I sought shelter on the leeward side of a parked truck, I remained completely dry. After the rainfall subsided, I remained on US 2 and followed the rain cloud eleven miles to Shelby, located some seventy-five miles north of Great Falls on Interstate 15.

At five-thirty, as I stopped at the truck stop near the interstate exit, I faced an important decision. I knew there was a campground nearby, but the idea of camping lacked appeal. I picked up the telephone book and flipped through the Yellow Pages, looking under "churches" and "clergy." I found a listing for Reverend Grover Briggs, pastor of the Community United Methodist Church.

When I called the parsonage, Rev. Briggs answered. I introduced myself and asked, "Would it be possible for me to sleep in your church tonight? A spot on the floor would be fine."

"Sure thing," he said, speaking in a deep drawl. "By the way, I just started fixing supper. Would you care to join us?" Before long I found myself at the door of his house. After parking the bicycle in the hallway of the church next door, I cleaned up for dinner.

The Briggses are a two-career family. Beth Briggs, a nurse, came home around six-thirty, exhausted from a long day of work. Grover Briggs had dinner waiting, capably balancing his responsibilities as pastor and houseparent. We enjoyed a relaxing evening together, swapping stories and exchanging hopes for a better world. We discussed numerous topics, including the Church's role in society, the status and social conditions of Native Americans (among whom Rev. Briggs had worked), and the presence of anti-ballistic missile installations in the states of Montana and North Dakota.

Later that night, as I prepared to sleep in the church, I became alarmed to hear the sound of water running in the basement. But as soon as I considered getting up to check it out, the sound stopped. Then it resumed. This went on for some time. I finally climbed out of the sleeping bag and walked cautiously toward the stairs. I checked the side door and found that it didn't lock properly. Rev. Briggs had told me stories of transients he had found sleeping in the church, so when I noticed a light on downstairs I was certain I had company. I tiptoed down the stairs and looked into several rooms, but I couldn't find anyone. Was someone hiding? I stood quietly for a few moments, my heart pounding. At that point the sound of running water resumed and I discovered that it was coming from a malfunctioning toilet. The noise was caused by an occasional surge of water that flowed into the toilet. The sound of water moving through the pipes in the basement, coupled with the stillness of the church, had played games on my overactive mind. Having solved the mystery, I returned to my makeshift bed on the floor of the Sunday School room, determined to make the best of the situation, though I couldn't dispel the nagging thought that an intruder might actually be lurking nearby.

The following morning I awoke at six o'clock, having promised Rev. Briggs that I would join him for an early morning ecumenical Bible study at a local café. He laughed when I told him about my concerns during the night and assured me that transients looked for lodging in local churches only during the cold winter months. I recalled the Scripture verse: "Have no anxiety about anything"; in retrospect, it was clear that I had been anxious about nothing.

As we sat together around the large table in the café, my companions listened intently to the story of the trek and my involvement with Habitat. Each one was supportive, including the gentleman who responded, bluntly, "I hate 'thons': phone-a-thons, jog-a-thons, walk-a-thons, skate-a-thons, dance-a-thons. Thons 'use' people, especially young people."

I agreed I didn't care for pressured events either, particularly for the hype that often accompanies them. I assured him my journey was not a "thon."

"In my case," I added, "I volunteered to do something I enjoyed doing. And I feel the trek is a good way for people to focus on a worthwhile cause. In my estimation, Christians without a cause are like people without a heart. Furthermore," I concluded, "I believe there is no greater privilege than to be used by God. If anyone is being used by this trek it is me, by my own choice."

It was an honest exchange of ideas, given in Christian love. The fellowship hour was not over until I received my speaker's fee: a large order of pancakes.

Stage 12 (August 11): Shelby to Havre – 106 miles

By nine o'clock I was back on US 2, my route for the next seven days. The map indicated that straight stretches of road lay ahead, and I envisioned relaxed riding after such hard labor in the mountains. But what I presumed to be straight and flat terrain was an unending succession of small hills, which I traversed with tiresome regularity. From each hilltop I saw the upcoming stretch of road, identical to the one I had just passed; no houses or trees, simply grassland as far as the eye could see.

In Montana—"Big Sky Country"—the disproportion between man and nature is so great that a person can be crushed by the vastness and solitude. Like a searing wind, the environment draws nourishment from exposed, unsuspecting creatures, absorbing them into itself.

A line from a popular song by the musical group "Kansas" came to mind: "Dust in the wind; all we are is dust in the wind."[1] To pedal this vast expanse alone, without a reservoir of physical and spiritual resources, is to become that cosmic particle of dust, blowing helplessly in the great western wind.

Someone I met earlier, who knew I was cycling across the country, had said: "I could never do that, bike alone. I don't like myself that much." That statement contained several truths, two of which became evident to me as I cycled across the Great Plains: (1) one gets to know oneself intimately on a solo cross-country bicycle trip (and you'd better like what you see), and (2) one must have self-respect and confidence, for along the way what is shallow and phony will be exposed.

It was late in the summer when I pedaled east of the Rockies, and I encountered no cyclists in that part of Montana, no supportive riders to accompany me. I would be crossing the wilderness alone. As I rode the "High Line," as the route along the railroad is called, only an occasional whistle from freight trains and the predictably small towns broke the monotony. Towns named Dunkirk, Devon, Lothair, Inverness, Rudyard, Hingham, Kremlin, Havre, Harlem, Zurich, Malta, and Glasgow spoke of

---

1. Words by Kerry Livgren, Don Kirshner Music (Blackwood Music Publishing); cf. Psalm 18:42.

the early days, when settlers came, many from overseas, with inexpensive one-way tickets and the promise of a good life on productive land.

Between 1887 and 1893, James J. Hill, the "Empire Builder," employed thousands of workers to complete a railroad between Minot, North Dakota and Seattle, Washington. Cowtowns arose first, places like Havre, Shelby, and Culbertson; then came the farmers, on the heels of technological breakthroughs in agricultural implements. Favorable weather and productivity raised initial hopes, but drought followed, accompanied by heavy winds that turned the topsoil to dust. And grasshoppers stripped whatever survived. Economic depression and natural calamities came in waves between 1918 and the 1930s. Homesteaders left, towns folded, and much of the region reverted to pastureland.

Today's ride was hardly memorable. It had been a day of struggle, a weary, monotonous exertion against the harsh elements. The primary culprit was the wind; unlike yesterday's favorable tailwind, today's wind had blown from the southeast. I struggled against it all day. When one cycles a hundred miles in Montana into a headwind, with temperatures in the nineties, one feels like the terrain looks: desiccated and drained. That's how I felt as I entered Havre.

But there was a beneficial side. The heat was a dry heat, not like that of the East Coast, where a ninety-degree day is usually accompanied by high humidity. And my outlook was positive. It seemed fair to alternate favorable and unfavorable days.

I felt encouraged by the prospects awaiting me at Havre. Rev. Bob Armstrong from Pennsylvania had arranged lodging in advance, and tomorrow was the first scheduled rest day. I looked forward to a time of recuperation and relaxation.

Stage 13 (August 12): DAY OFF

My host for the next two days was Mrs. Sharon Clawson. She sounded friendly and sympathetic when I spoke with her on the telephone. I would be staying in the youth lounge of a church for two nights, but I would eat at her home, with her family. When I arrived at the Van Orsdel Methodist Church, I was taken to the Fireside Room, a comfortable room complete with sofa and television. Given my circumstances, the setting seemed extravagant.

It was Friday night, the closing weekend at the Hill County Fair, and both Sharon and her husband Sam, a recruiter for the National Guard, had duties at the fair. Yet they found time to fit me into their busy schedules and to make me welcome in their home.

Sharon took one look at me and decided that my metabolism was traveling faster than my bicycle. The physical demands of the trip had stripped me of any reserves, and I hadn't taken in enough calories to compensate. I was below my usual slim weight, thinner than thin. Normally I explain my appearance by remarking, "I need to eat a lot just to stay thin." This time the truth was excruciatingly obvious. Sharon took it upon herself to remedy my condition within thirty-six hours. And did I eat!

That evening I returned to the Van Orsdel church and immediately felt at home in my attractive surroundings. A glass-enclosed case in the foyer held mementos and told the story of the Reverend William Van Orsdel, known fondly as Brother Van. This circuit-riding cleric overcame many hardships after he settled on the Montana frontier in 1872. In addition to being a brilliant preacher, he helped found schools and hospitals. The church's name memorialized his remarkable career.

The following day was a Saturday, and I slept in. What a luxury! After a late breakfast with the Clawsons I enjoyed an afternoon at a nearby pool. Saturday night was Rodeo Night at the fair, and I marveled at the thrills provided by genuine cowboys and cowgirls in action. The contestants, some of whom came from out of state, impressed the audience with their skills. I especially enjoyed the crowds and the noise, after the silence of the plains. Watching eight- and nine-year-olds perform daredevil stunts such as bareback sheep riding and lamb wrestling added to the fun.

But the culminating event of the evening did not occur at the rodeo. Instead it took place at the Optimist dunking booth, where Sergeant Sam Clawson sat in his dress uniform, bracing for a dunking by impatient recruits who had waited a long time for this moment of retribution; even the Clawson family members lacked compassion. And I, their guest, decided to follow suit. It only took me two tosses to dislodge the sergeant from his precarious perch.

Stage 14 (August 13): Havre to Malta – 92 miles

After my brief day of rest and recuperation, it was time to hit the pavement again. Sunday's ride was a tedious, ninety-two miler. Thankfully my accommodations for the night were set. I had called ahead and had been invited to stay in the home of a Lutheran pastor in the town of Malta. Freed of concern about lodging, I did what I had come to do—work.

To my dismay, I noticed that the wind was coming out of the southeast again; there would be no tailwinds today. I tried to think positively about the task before me: the day off had revived me, physically and spiritually; I hadn't been sick on the trek; the mountains were behind me; the temperature was bearable; and sometime during that day's ride I would pedal the one thousandth mile of the trek. The day bore promise.

Also, as a solo cyclist, I found most motorists to be supportive and friendly. I had chosen a good year to cycle through Montana and the Pacific Northwest, for six northern states were enjoying centennial celebrations during 1989 and 1990: Washington, Idaho, Wyoming, Montana, and North and South Dakota. Citizens from these states were putting their best foot forward, sharing goodwill with visitors.

As I left Havre, I noticed a slow-moving stream alongside the route. The Milk River began its course on the east slope of Glacier Park, flowing parallel to Route 2 for 200 miles before it merged with the Missouri River at a point just below Fort Peck Dam. Meriwether Lewis, of the Lewis and Clark expedition, had described the river as being the color of tea, with the addition of a tablespoon of milk; hence its name, Milk River.

At one point, as I stopped for a break along its bank, I was alarmed to find mosquitoes rapidly covering my legs. Remembering the caution given by those two cyclists in Tiger, Washington, I also recalled reading in the Lewis and Clark journals about mosquitoes and other insects so thick that rifle barrels became clouded and gunsights were rendered useless. I made a hasty retreat, noting that the mosquitoes would not bother me while I pedaled. Montana became one of several states along the route for which the mosquito qualified as the state bird.

Aside from the meandering Milk River, another natural phenomenon asserted its presence as I left Havre: the Bear Paw Mountains. This landmark is associated with a tragic chapter in the history of the American Indians. It was here, on an October day in 1877, that Chief Joseph and his Nez Perce people made their final stand. This small band from Idaho, revolting against encroachment by whites, fought a running battle with army troops. Heading towards refuge in Canada, Chief Joseph finally slowed the pace, after a 1,800-mile trek across the Rockies. Near Chinook, less than a day's march from refuge in Canada, he was surprised by the troops of Colonel Nelson Miles and was forced to surrender after a four-day fight. Chief Joseph was taken to Fort Buford, where the Yellowstone and Missouri Rivers converge, and then to Fort Leavenworth, Kansas, before his exile to the Colville Reservation in eastern Washington. An impressive diorama of the surrender can be seen at the H. Earl Clack Museum, located at the Hill County fairgrounds in Havre. Chief Joseph's surrender marked the end of Montana's Indian wars, following the disaster of Custer and his Seventh Cavalry on the banks of the Little Big Horn in 1876.

The final chapter in the Indian Wars of the nineteenth century ended on December 29, 1890, with the tragic massacre of a band of Oglala Sioux at Wounded Knee, located in what is now the Pine Ridge Reservation in South Dakota.

According to my diary, I "crawled" into Malta at six-forty that evening, a victim of the day's forced march. I identified with Chief Joseph's ordeal and was eager to surrender. My average speed had been twelve and a half miles an hour, not much faster than the climb along "Going-to-the-Sun," across the Continental Divide. This was the lowest average I ever achieved for a day's ride. But no one called for my surrender; instead, a warm meal and caring fellowship awaited me at the home of Rev. Brad and Diane Brauer. We talked until midnight, and that night I slept in a comfortable bed in my own room—my first such experience since leaving home three weeks earlier. I appreciated the pampering.

In Malta, I made two telephone calls that further encouraged me. The first was to a minister in Glasgow, who assured me of a place to stay the following night, and the second was to Susan and my children, who were visiting relatives in Colorado.

The Brauers provided me with some background information on Malta. From 1870 to 1900, the town had been the center of a cattle empire that reached to Havre and the Canadian border. In addition, this small town also claimed Charles M. Russell, Montana's most famous painter, who produced many of his pictures in and around Malta. It was his picture of a starving range cow, "Waiting for a Chinook" (also known as "The Last of Five Thousand"), that first won him recognition as an artist.

Stage 15 (August 14): Malta to Glasgow – 72 miles

As I awoke that Monday morning, I felt optimistic. Today's ride was only seventy-two miles, and I had been assured lodging for the next two

nights. In addition, I confidently expected the wind to change directions in the near future. For three days it had blown out of a southern or
southeastern direction. But my heart skipped a beat when the morning's
forecast predicted strong winds, twenty to twenty-five miles an hour, out
of the southeast. Without examining the map, I knew that today's journey
would be into the wind, again. And that meant only one thing, agony!

The comments in my diary that day were terse: "headwind all day—
really tough biking!" The day's hardships also took their toll on the bicycle,
as the right crank became unstable again. At first the wobble was bearable,
but after a full day of pedaling the uneven stroke became intolerable, like
Chinese water torture. Anyone can endure an occasional drop of water,
but not continuously, eight hours a day.

Self-accusing thoughts began to plague me. I pondered my earlier
decision to relinquish my tools to Susan. Having expected to find bicycle
shops along the route, now I knew that that certainly was not the case in
eastern Montana. I wondered whether there was a purpose—something
greater than a coincidence—behind the fact that the bicycle was malfunctioning on the most remote stretch of the trip.

Cycling across the country is warfare. The contest begins on the
physical level, as the body fights to overcome pain, fatigue, and natural
challenges such as the elements and the terrain. I had expected that level
of conflict, and I felt I could survive the battle, with proper rest and the
use of techniques such as stretching and self-massage.

But like a chess match, the physical level was preliminary to a deeper
conflict, to a spiritual contest of wills fought in the arena of the mind,
the emotions, and the spirit. The relentless wind had become a cunning
opponent, exploiting areas of weakness, searching out my Achilles' heel.
This was not a foe I could defeat physically. My fists were useless against
it, so I fought with words, shouting forcibly.

Continuous days of biking into the wind had deprived me of joy
and even eliminated the challenge of cycling. As I saw it, this was all-out
war! Invoking the biblical principle, "If God is for us, who is against us?" I
found it expedient to bring my spiritual resources into the struggle. After
all, wasn't I God's child? And wasn't God in control of the wind and other
natural forces? Then why such abnormal circumstances, why such unfair
conditions? Did God care about me and my plight? These were extreme
thoughts, but so were the circumstances. I was unaccustomed to such a
tenacious foe. Because this was an unfamiliar wind, it was mysterious,

and I was learning that as a modern human I didn't fare well in the presence of the unknown.

Eventually, feeling overwhelmed and abandoned, I cried out, "God, are you listening? Are you listening to anyone?" This despairing accusation, though increasing my sense of guilt, became therapeutic. It was an open expression of honesty.

Yesterday I had thought about Abraham, the "father of faith," and about his obedient faithfulness and how he harnessed uncertainty and disappointment and learned from his trials. Yesterday I had been optimistic, ready to learn from nature's lessons. But today my thoughts were on Job, the innocent sufferer, who demanded justice.

Job is generally remembered as a patient person, even under trial, as one who never sinned or charged God with wrong (Job 1:21–22). That, of course, is the emphasis in the narrative section of the book of Job (in the opening chapters and in the epilogue; 42:7–17). But in the poetic section (3:1–42:6), written after the original account, Job experiences the full gamut of emotions: shock, anger, depression, and lament. He curses the day of his birth (3:1). He is angry and embittered (7:11) and considers God to be unfair (9:15), insensitive to the plight of the needy (8:22–23.), a treacherous assailant (7:20; 16:12–14), and his adversary (16:9; 31:35).

These are tremendous accusations: Job doubts, rebels, and shouts defiance at God. He expresses extreme feelings of estrangement. But at stake is his relationship with God. Job is fighting to overcome that estrangement with all the weapons at his disposal.

As I recall the lessons of that day of cycling, I am aware that experiences such as these are like spiritual wake-up calls. As we examine the circumstances of our lives, most of us find that in our early years we are aided by favorable tailwinds. Then midlife comes, its purpose being to prepare us for the uncertainties of old age and that final foe, death. My trek—a metaphor for the journey of life—serves as a reminder that we humans cannot venture into the headwinds and wilderness experiences that surely await us without adequate resources: physical, mental, emotional, and spiritual. And those resources are byproducts of our experiences and the lessons they teach us. The experiences we avoid or deem most unhelpful are sometimes our most effective and enduring mentors.

When I finally arrived in Glasgow, it was late in the day. A glance at the cyclocomputer revealed that my average speed had been slightly over twelve miles an hour, lower than yesterday! Strangely, however, I felt a measure of victory, for I had reached my destination. And I had done so by subdividing the task into bite-size pieces; towns, hilltops, bridges, signs, historic markers, crossroads, lakes, and railroad tracks had become milestones, and I felt a sense of accomplishment crossing even the slightest marker. Inch by inch, that's how I reached Glasgow.

Once in town, I headed directly for a service station. My first priority was to secure the bike's crank. Assuming that I had not tightened the bolt sufficiently on previous occasions, I determined to supply enough torque this time to make it hold. Only after doing so did I proceed to the local Methodist church, where I spent the night sleeping comfortably on a couch in the pastor's study.

The following morning I discovered that the wind direction had not changed from the previous day and that in addition, it was the strongest wind I had faced thus far. I remembered the advice someone had given me earlier, when I had complained about the constant headwinds in the plains: "Why don't you turn around and head in the opposite direction?"

The proposal seemed perversely attractive, but I hadn't come this far to travel in circles. My course was set. The path of least resistance was not the way home—physically or spiritually.

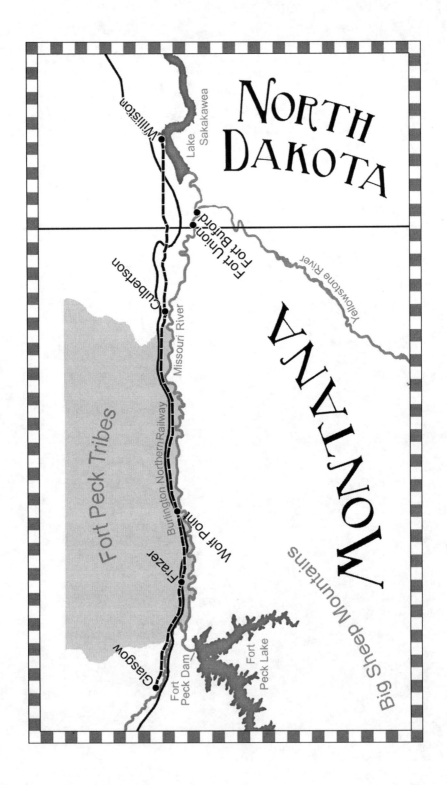

8

Breakdown: The Spiritual Watershed

STAGES 16–17: EASTERN MONTANA— GLASGOW TO WILLISTON, NORTH DAKOTA [144 MILES]

Stage 16 (August 15): Glasgow to Wolf Point – 52 miles

Today's ride was supposed to be easy. My destination was Wolf Point, Montana, a distance of only fifty-two miles. I had considered a detour to Fort Peck Dam, the largest hydraulic earthfill dam in the world, but a check on the wind convinced me otherwise. Today's goal had to be simple: reach Wolf Point. Bucking a twenty-five-mile-per-hour wind yielded only twenty miles by noon, an unacceptable distance for a cross-country cyclist.

Progress was stymied by another factor: the bolt used for tightening the pedal crank was not holding. I needed a socket wrench, but where could I locate such a tool in this wasteland? I was about to enter the one hundred-mile-long Fort Peck Indian Reservation, and there were no automotive services between here and Wolf Point.

I focused on the mechanical problem. What was causing the crank to wobble? Could it be a bent chainring? At the first town along the reservation I found a convenience store, but they had no socket wrenches. Eventually a Native American pulled up in a pickup and offered me the use of his toolbox. He didn't have the size wrench I needed, but he did have a hammer, with which I could straighten out the chainring if it was bent. When he took the hammer from behind the seat, I recoiled in surprise. This was no ordinary hammer; its two-foot-long handle made it look more like a weapon than a hammer. How ironic, I thought. A hun-

73

dred years ago we might have been adversaries, and the tool would most likely have been a tomahawk. Now this Indian came as an ally, ready to assist a white man in distress. The role reversal got my attention. I was able to remove the chainring, but after careful examination I could find nothing wrong with it. I didn't know what to do next; I had a problem but no solution.

Continuing along the highway for fifteen miles, I spotted the village of Frazer. The only sign of life in town was the grocery store. The clerk, a bright young man, took an interest in my plight. He looked through some tools in a drawer and pulled out a socket wrench. Unfortunately, most of the sockets were missing, including the one I needed for the recessed bolt.

As I pondered my predicament, I noticed Indians entering the store. Realizing that this might be my one opportunity to observe life on a reservation, I paid particular attention as young children entered the store in clusters. They seemed to want only one thing, candy. And they were determined to get the most for their money. One pensive five-year-old took about ten minutes to decide how to spend his dollar. This was a daily routine for the children, coming to the store and leaving with handfuls of candy. My curiosity turned to concern. What were these impressionable children learning from this routine? Would their craving for sweets lead to adult dependence upon fast food, cigarettes, and alcohol? Worse yet, would it lead to drugs or other abusive addictions?

My thoughts were interrupted by sounds of construction work coming from the building next door. I hoped the renovations might provide benefits to the community, something of value to the youth that loitered about. My optimistic hopes were dashed when I learned that a bar and poolroom were under construction. My concern turned to anger as I contemplated the long-range prospects for this community. I realized that the anger and indignation I felt about the Indians on the reservation mirrored my own predicament. For the moment, at least, the prognosis seemed bleak for all of us.

By this point the bicycle crank was practically useless. It was so ineffective that I considered thumbing a ride to Wolf Point. But I quickly set that idea aside because I was convinced that my trek had a higher purpose; it could not end in futility or compromise. I decided instead to continue pedaling, hoping that the day's trials might act as a sounding board for "the still small voice of God." Yesterday had been a day of resentment, of blaming God and the wind. The time for counterpunching was over. Today I would listen, that I might grow.

Although the Rockies were behind me, I felt as if I were still climbing a mountain, only this one was invisible. One of the reasons I had decided to travel eastward was to take advantage of the prevailing winds, which I considered generally favorable in that direction. But for days, adverse conditions had predominated. The obstinate winds had become an obstacle greater than climbing the Rockies, greater even than that fifty-eight-mile climb to the summit at Washington Pass in the Cascades. Pedaling against the wind in the plains was like climbing an endless mountain. All day I climbed, without ever reaching the top. There were no descents, no moments to coast, nothing to alter my mood. Like Sisyphus, I pushed the stone up the mountain, only to have it roll back upon me as I neared the top. It was time to let go; I had to stop pushing that stone and listen.

From the start, the trek had been my idea. No one had forced me into it. And one of my goals was to undertake a journey of magnitude, a journey conducive to spiritual development.[1] I felt that God could calm the wind and provide endless tailwinds, but I also knew that such intervention would prevent me from fulfilling my deepest yearnings and needs. God promises guidance and companionship, not idyllic natural conditions. In fact, the Scriptures attest to a rather different reality: "The wind blows where it wills" (John 3:8).

Like the ancient Israelites, I had come to the wilderness and found a mountain. The Bible speaks of this mountain as a place of adversity but also as a place of encounter and revelation. The Psalmist refers to this experience as "the desolate pit" (Psalm 40:2), "the depths" (Psalm 130:1), or "the valley of deep darkness" (Psalm 23:4, note). There was a time in the Prophet Elijah's life when he too traveled to the mountain. And it was there, on the mountain of Horeb (Sinai), that he heard the still small voice:

> And behold, the Lord passed by, and a great and strong wind rent the mountains,
>
> and broke in pieces the rocks before the Lord, but the Lord was not in the wind;

1. According to Arnold Toynbee, nations and individuals thrive when they contend with crises or challenges. This is the basic premise in his *A Study of History* (London: Oxford, 1934 to 1961). Jimmy and Roselyn Carter promote this perspective in *Everything to Gain*, 191.

and after the wind an earthquake, but the Lord was not in the
earthquake;

and after the earthquake a fire, but the Lord was not in the fire;
and after the fire a still small voice (1 Kings 19:11-12).

When Elijah finally heard the voice of the Lord, the resultant message transformed not only him but a widening circle around him as well,
including Elisha, his partner in ministry, and the persons of power in his
immediate world.

That message hit home. Did I need an earthquake or a fire to hear
the "still small voice," or would the wind suffice? I decided to listen. And
as I set aside the natural voices competing for my attention, I heard another voice, declaring words not of my own choosing: "When you and I
agree on a plan, nothing can thwart it. Today may be tough; today you
may experience inconvenience and setback, but I will provide a way. Yield
to my strategy, for my plan will succeed." I was comforted by these words
of assurance, though I had no idea what the strategy might be. That would
be manifested in due time.

For the moment, the message seemed to be epitomized in the word
P-A-T-I-E-N-C-E: not a patience of resignation but a patience of perseverance. This sort of patience, when it yokes vision with action, prays,
"Thy kingdom come, Thy will be done," and then immediately begins
living out the answer to that prayer.[2] Patience is essential to all growth,
whether personal or spiritual, for God uses patience to shape and equip
us for ministry (Hebrews 6:11–12).

In *The Purpose-Driven Life*, Rick Warren uses the word SHAPE as
an acrostic to help us understand how God participates in our shaping
process:

Spiritual gifts; *Heart; Abilities; Personality; Experience.*

When Warren discusses the topic of experience, and how experiences shape us, he argues that it is our painful experiences that God uses
most to prepare us for ministry and for life. "God never wastes a hurt," he

---

2. St. Paul has a lot to say about patience. For him it is part of a process: ". . . we rejoice
in our sufferings, knowing that suffering produces [patient] endurance, and endurance
produces character, and character produces hope, and hope does not disappoint us . . ."
(Romans 5:3–5a). Elsewhere he adds, "Base your happiness on your hope in Christ. When
trials come, endure them patiently; steadfastly maintain the habit of prayer" (Romans
12:12, J. B. Phillips). This kind of patience is active and transforming; it is faith at work!

writes. "In fact, your greatest ministry will most likely come out of your greatest hurt."[3] At this point the skeptic within us asks, "But what if things don't get better? What if they get worse?" The answer is, they will get better, if we are willing to wait and never to give up.

Robert H. Schuller, host of the Hour of Power television program and longtime pastor of the Crystal Cathedral in Garden Grove, California, crafted an analogy in his Possibility Thinkers Creed: "When faced with a mountain, I will not quit! I will keep on striving until I climb over, find a pass through, tunnel underneath, or simply stay . . . and turn the mountain into a miracle, with God's help." The Psalmist knows that waiting upon the Lord imparts strength and increases courage. And even if circumstances don't improve the way we expect, they will get better. When we commit our ways unto the Lord, God will bring them to pass (Psalm 37:4–5; Proverbs 16:3).

Tailwinds rarely evoke wisdom, but insights flow freely from the watershed atop life's invisible mountains.

Though I lacked the mechanical tools to repair my bicycle, I acquired two indispensable tools on that mountaintop: (1) patience, and (2) hopeful imagination. These tools go together, for patience is the key that unlocks the lock to hopeful imagination, and hopeful imagination opens the door to God's better ideas. The secret of these tools, as with all God's gifts, is in their use. Unused, they have no value.

As I applied newly discovered insights to my situation, I examined the circumstances: a balky bicycle, overpowering headwinds, a socket wrench without sockets, no services between here and Wolf Point, and a bicycle crank that might fall off at any moment. There was little room here for optimism or ingenuity.

Nevertheless, I made the decision not to accept a lift to Wolf Point. Tomorrow, if circumstances did not improve, I might consider such a possibility. But today I would simply be patient, wait upon the Lord, and keep pedaling.

That afternoon, patience "paid off." Prior to my departure from Frazer, a young Native American came by in his pickup. I asked him if he knew where I might find a socket to fit the wrench I had borrowed.

3. (Grand Rapids, MI: Zondervan, 2002) 246–47; for his discussion of SHAPE, consult chapters 30–33, pp. 234–56.

He told me he had some sockets in his house. When he returned, he carried a nine-sixteenth-inch socket, precisely the one I needed. That socket and the store clerk's wrench got me back on the road with renewed optimism, and I was able to reach Wolf Point by four o'clock. But the average speed, ten and a half miles per hour, was a testament to the day's colossal struggle. It was my slowest recorded ride to date.

My hosts for the evening, Rev. James and Bonnie Coats, were a godsend. Congenial, helpful, and inspiring, they were just what I needed after my D-day experience. That evening, after serving me a charcoal-cooked steak dinner, Rev. Coats placed himself at my disposal. He contacted a retired gentleman in town who repaired bicycles, and an hour later my bicycle was upside down in his back yard, a piece of cardboard providing the base for the makeshift workshop. Though he lacked the proper tools, the clever repairman managed to remove the bottom bracket by using a hammer and chisel. His diagnosis proved accurate: the bearings were worn. But since they were housed in a sealed unit, the entire unit needed to be replaced. With a clientele limited to youngsters with American-made bikes, the old man's stock contained only used parts. He wasn't prepared to replace bearings on fancy foreign bicycles with triple chainrings. And he assured me that no one in eastern Montana carried the part I needed. The closest service was in Williston, North Dakota, one hundred miles away, and he didn't believe the crankset would last long enough to get me there.

We put the bicycle together as best we could, in the dark, with the help of a flashlight. Because we had used improper tools, the cranks were in worse condition now than when we had started. But at least I knew the remedy. Insight is half the battle.

Stage 17 (August 16): Wolf Point to Williston – 92 miles

Rev. Coats volunteered to drive me to Culbertson, half way to Williston, in his pickup camper, but only if I was willing to arise early. I agreed readily. Surely I could cycle the last forty-four miles to Williston on my own. I awoke at five-thirty, and after a hearty breakfast, I secured the bicycle inside the camper and left for Culbertson.

After several miles I remembered that I had left all of my water bottles in the Coats's freezer, where I had stored them overnight, so I said, "Jim, we have to go back."

His firm, immediate reply, "We can't do that," caught me by surprise.

I knew he was pressed for time, but surely he was aware that I couldn't continue without water bottles.

"You'll be able to find some bottles down the road," he added, matter-of-factly.

That answer brought me little comfort, until I noticed the twinkle in his eyes. And when we arrived in Culbertson, the bottles materialized. Jim had remembered to bring them. Lighthearted moments like these made the strenuous portions of the trek more bearable.

From Culbertson I made two telephone calls to Williston and was assured assistance. Rev. Chuck Mansfield, interim pastor of First Union Church, felt quite certain that he could find overnight accommodations. And when I called the Williston Coast to Coast Hardware store, the salesman at the bicycle shop guaranteed assistance. Now all I had to do was get to Williston.

But that was no simple matter. Today's wind, a vicious crosswind, struck me like a fist, blowing stronger than the day before, with gusts around thirty-five miles an hour. And when those gusts hit, I had to grasp my handlebars with an iron grip, fighting for control like a novice. The heavy bicycle reeled under the strain, barely clinging to the pavement. And the harder I pedaled, the more fragile the crankset became. My fastest speed was eight miles per hour. Three miles beyond Culbertson, I dismounted, unable to proceed. It was time to stop the madness.

My only option was to stick out my thumb and hope for a ride. The option proved to be quite embarrassing. There I stood, next to my bicycle, thumbing a ride! Those who passed by must have thought I was joking. Two pickups did stop, but the drivers informed me they weren't going very far. Then, for over half an hour, no one passed. I was puzzled by this lack of traffic on *the* major highway across northern Montana and North Dakota. There had to be traffic! My head began to spin as things whirled out of focus.

Finally a highway patrol car appeared. The officer explained that traffic was being held up for a truck convoy that carried an oversized load down the two-lane highway. Soon I heard the roar of two huge trucks traveling side by side at a speed of fifty miles an hour. The ground shook as they thundered by, occupying both lanes. It was an impressive sight, quite a contrast to my own sense of powerlessness.

Another thirty minutes went by before three Canadians stopped in their pickup, hauling a fifth-wheel trailer. They apologized for the lack of room, with the trailer hitched halfway up the pickup bed. The presence of a large built-in toolbox left little room in the back of the pickup, but I managed to wedge the bicycle in sideways, supporting it from my crouched position above the toolbox.

About an hour later I arrived on the outskirts of Williston, wind-blown and bone-weary, but relieved to be in a major city at last, with a modern bicycle shop and a qualified mechanic nearby. I arrived at the bicycle shop a few minutes before noon, expecting that my ordeal would soon be over. But my hopes were quickly dashed. The salesman had misunderstood the nature of my request, and he was unable to assist me. In addition, his stock of bicycles, parts, and tools was limited to American-made bicycles. And his was the only bicycle shop in town! I was stunned by this development. Was there any way out of my predicament?

I cycled to the manse, surprised at the ease with which I could pedal the sheltered streets of a city. Though the wind was still raging in the open plains, here in town conditions were relatively calm. Rev. Mansfield was eating a late lunch when I arrived, and he invited me to join him. This young pastor had contacted Clarence and Vern Rau, and they had agreed to provide me with accommodations for the night. Rev. Mansfield drove me to their upholstery shop, on the outskirts of town, for introductions. The Raus promptly took me into their confidence and provided me with a key to their house. Clarence even offered me the use of his pickup, which I declined. The bicycle was adequate for transportation around town.

On the way back to the manse, as Rev. Mansfield and I explored my options, an idea occurred to me, a "hopeful idea." I decided to call Bike Nashbar in Ohio, the largest bicycle mail-order dealer in the United States. Surely they could help me, especially since I had purchased my bicycle through them. If they had the necessary part, I knew it could be shipped out almost immediately. But my optimism was curtailed by the operator's response, "I'm sorry, we carry most bicycle parts, but we don't sell cranksets."

I couldn't believe my ears. It was as if someone were saying, "We can solve any problem but yours." I knew there was no truth to that. There had to be a solution. I put my "possibility thinking" into high gear and recalled the expression, "The greater the problem, the greater the opportunity." So before the salesman could hang up, I asked the next logical question, "Do you know anyone who sells the crankset I need?" There was a moment of awkward silence before he volunteered the name of a competitor. I was thrilled to hear the name, for not only was I familiar with this East Coast distributor, but I also had an account with them.

The next telephone call resulted in the best news I had heard in days, "Yes, we do have a triple crankset. Do you want it with English, Italian, or French threading?" Well, what kind of threading does a Japanese bicycle require? Why wasn't there Japanese threading? I made an educated guess, "English," and hoped for the best.

I was told that Federal Express would ship the part, which normally meant next-day service, but since the parts shop was already closed for the day, I could expect the shipment to arrive in two days. Although I should have been satisfied with that explanation, I wasn't pleased with the idea of a two-day delay in Williston. I was scheduled to meet Wayne Armstrong in Fargo on Monday, August 21, five days from then. And Fargo was 450 miles away, quite a challenge even with favorable winds. Additional delays would make it practically impossible to arrive on time.

I looked at my watch. It was not quite five o'clock on the East Coast. I explained that because my trip was a fundraising trek, it was imperative that I stay on schedule. The receptionist paused for a moment, and then asked me to remain on the line. A few moments later I heard her say, "Your part is being shipped right now. You'll receive it sometime tomorrow." As I hung up I uttered a quick prayer of thanks; I felt more hopeful than I had in a long time. With God's help, I was finding a way over the mountain.

My stay in Williston was a faith-building experience, for the Raus as well as for me. As Vern Rau wrote later, "Your visit came when our family was walking in one of those valleys in our journey of faith." I had felt the same way after five days of headwinds in the plains of Montana.

That night, as we gathered around the dinner table, the Raus decided to drive me to Fort Union, a nineteenth-century trading post at the confluence of the Yellowstone and Missouri Rivers, twenty-four miles southwest of Williston.

The trading post, reconstructed by the National Park Service after four years of work and at a cost of nearly one million dollars, had been completed recently. Both North Dakota and Montana had sanctioned the grand dedication as a centennial event.

This historic fort, built in 1829 by the American Fur Company, shaped and controlled the trading economy of the Northern Plains for almost forty years. Indians came from all directions: Mandans, Hidatsa, and Arikara up the Missouri, and Crows down the Yellowstone; Assiniboines came south, Sioux north, and Chippewa west; and Crees came from Canada. It is believed that during this period more Indians came to trade at Fort Union than to any other frontier post.[4]

We were disappointed to find the fort closed when we arrived, but we were able to walk around its perimeter, impressed by the stone bastions and twenty-foot-high palisades. We paused at the square where trading took place in times of sickness or when hostilities prevented Indians from entering the post itself. It was the flow of whiskey, though prohibited, which caused the fort's initial outstanding success. But it was whiskey as well that led to deteriorating conditions between Indians and whites, and to the eventual dismantling of the fort. Its materials were then used to build Fort Buford, two miles away, a location best remembered as the sight of the surrender of Chief Sitting Bull in 1881, after the bloody Battle of the Little Big Horn. My tour continued with a visit to Fort Buford. A few original features remained, including a stone powder magazine, large officers' quarters, and the post cemetery.

A great deal of American history was made at this busy crossroads, where innumerable vessels, wagon trains, and other means of transportation brought, then supplied, generations of traders and settlers to the northern plains. It didn't take much imagination to recall the era of Lewis and Clark and the brave traders, settlers, and Indians alike, caught between wilderness and civilization during a period of unprecedented change, who met, traded, and fought for supremacy here.

The walk through time concluded with a stunning spectacle in the heavens, as we witnessed a thunder and lightning show that accompanied the memorable sunset, always spectacular in open sky country. The evening's "light and sound" show culminated with the *coup de grâce*, a partial lunar eclipse. Nature seems to have the final say in the Great Plains.

---

4. An excellent work by a sympathetic eyewitness stationed at Fort Union for two decades is that of Edwin Thompson Denig, *Five Indian Tribes of the Upper Missouri*, edited by John C. Ewers (Norman, Oklahoma: University of Oklahoma Press, 1961).

The next day I planned a leisurely start, since Clarence anticipated that the package from the East Coast distributor wouldn't arrive until late in the day. I had just finished breakfast when he walked through the door, grinning and holding a package in his hands. The essential part had arrived fifteen minutes earlier, at nine thirty in the morning. It had come halfway across the continent, overnight; my miracle had begun.

With the arrival of the crankset, a second problem arose. I needed the proper tools for its installation. I did not intend to use a hammer and chisel to tighten this expensive crankset, as I had in Wolf Point. The potential for damage was too great. It was time to exercise "hopeful imagination" again. After several phone calls we located a mechanic named Matt Langdlan, who worked directly across the highway from the Rau's upholstery shop.

We placed the bicycle in Clarence's pickup and headed for the bicycle shop at the Coast to Coast Hardware store, where the attendant possessed a Park crank-arm extractor, an indispensable tool for use on cotterless cranks. I didn't know whether he would allow me to borrow it, but Clarence's presence gave me confidence. Clarence was well known in town, and his good reputation became my collateral.

It took Matt only an hour to complete the repairs. The bicycle was now in better condition than when I had left Pennsylvania, and the new crankcase was far superior to the original one. I had guessed correctly about the threading; the Japanese frame did require English threading, and nothing else would have worked. Matt replaced and tightened the new unit ingeniously, with the help of two punches, a wrench, and a special motorcycle tool. The total cost for labor? Free of charge.

I had witnessed a remarkable chain of events during the past twenty-four hours; surely all this was more than coincidental. Like the biblical account of Daniel's friends, I felt I had been thrown into a fiery furnace; but I had not endured it alone. And I knew I had a story to tell, for "God never wastes a hurt."

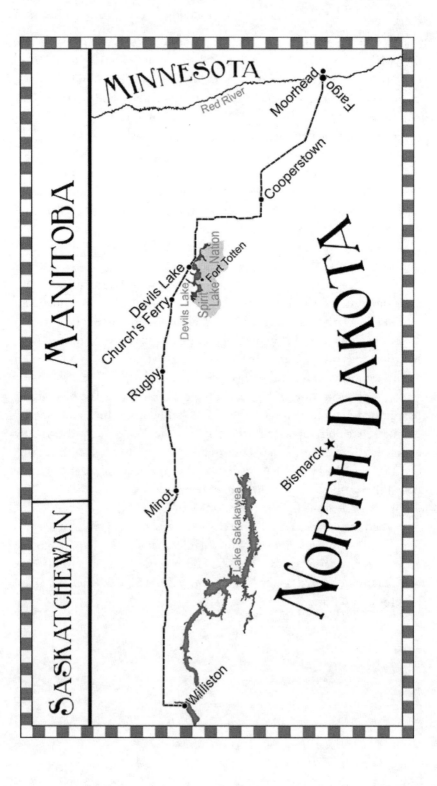

9

The Geographical Center

Stage 18 (August 17): Williston to Minot – 122 miles

To HELP KEEP ME on pace, the Raus offered to take me part way toward Minot that evening, after work. In the interim, I decided to pedal around town, excited to try out my refurbished bike and hoping to make up some lost mileage. I headed east along Route 1804, toward Lewis and Clark State Park on Lake Sakakawea. This was historic country, near the Mandan villages where Lewis and Clark had wintered in 1804–05. Here Sakakawea (Sacagawea), a young Shoshone Indian girl, had joined the Lewis and Clark expedition to the Pacific, proving indispensable as interpreter and guide across the Rockies.

The terrain along Rt. 1804, an extension of the Badlands, was the hilliest I had crossed since the Rockies. Once again the wind howled from the south, making for slow progress. But this time the bicycle was sound, and its steady response to my strongest pedaling restored my confidence.

The conditions, equally as brutal and challenging as those of the previous days, had somehow changed. The contest no longer had a spiritual dimension; it was simply a physical challenge now. The events surrounding the repair of the bicycle had effected a profound change in my attitude.

Upon my return to Williston, Clarence informed me that a friend of theirs had stopped by their shop that day on his way through town. He would be returning to Minot later that evening in his truck and he would be glad to take me to Minot, if I wanted to join him.

Whereas previously I would have turned such an offer down, now it made sense. Accepting the ride would put me back on schedule and allow me to reach Fargo in time for Wayne's arrival. I could make up the lost miles later.

Bidding farewell to the Raus, I was grateful for the faith and trust they had exhibited by taking me into their hearts and home on a moment's notice. They too had taken a risk, which was what this journey of faith was about.

Later, in a letter, Vern remarked, "I remember when Clarence told me our pastor had called, asking if we might provide housing for you. Clarence told me about your trip and then said, in effect, 'This person is a minister, but he could still be really weird.' It made me wonder as well, but then again, if we didn't meet you, we would never know. So we decided to be helpful and say 'yes.'" I found her concluding remarks particularly poignant: "As we talked it over afterwards we felt we had gained much through this experience. Neither of us would have wanted not to be a part of it. Seeing so many things fall into place was just what we needed. Who says miracles don't happen anymore?"

Since the trek's conception, I had been guaranteed lodging in Minot (rhymes with "why not"), North Dakota. Dr. Jonathan Wagner, an administrator at W & J College, had recently relocated to North Dakota to resume teaching at State College–Minot. Life out East had been too confining. He preferred the classroom to an administrator's office, and he loved the northern Great Plains and its style of life. When he heard of my trip, he assured me of lodging.

Upon arrival in Minot, I was pleased to learn that Dr. Wagner had not forgotten his promise. He had only recently moved into a farmhouse some twenty-five miles from Minot, and the moving van was still parked in his driveway. A former student of his was visiting when I called, so the two came to get me. I placed the bicycle in the back of the pickup, next to a large white dog, and joined the others in the front seat. Later, when I removed the bike, I had the distinct impression that the dog had mistaken my red panniers for fire hydrants.

Stage 19 (August 18): Minot to Devils Lake – 109 miles

The following morning I looked out the window for my customary check on the wind, and what I saw brought a huge smile to my face. Storms across the nation's midsection had changed the wind flow, and now, for the first time in a week, the wind was blowing from the northwest.

I left Minot with a slight tailwind, averaging a brisk eighteen miles an hour. Three and a half hours later I was in Rugby, fifty-seven miles from Minot. Rugby was a significant milestone, for a stone marker next to the highway indicated that I was standing at the "Geographical Center of North America," a claim established by a US Geological Survey in 1931.

Advancing to this point definitely gave me a psychological boost. I wasn't half way home, yet that morning's ride gave me the impression that I had crossed an invisible barrier. Recent foes—the wind, the bike, and the terrain—were metamorphosing into long-lost friends. Mountains, visible and invisible, were behind me, at least temporarily, and my mood was euphoric. But the euphoria was short-lived, for by the time I left Rugby the wind direction had changed, and it was in my face once again. This time rain accompanied it, not a heavy rain at first, but a steady drizzle. Since the moisture wasn't penetrating the panniers, I didn't bother to enclose my belongings in plastic bags, as I usually did during heavy rains. The succession of rainless days in the plains had lulled me into thinking that rainfall in North Dakota, especially during the summer months, would be light and sparse. That might be true for the western portion of the state, but not for the eastern section, which I was entering.

I decided to continue along Route 2, hoping to reach the town of Devils Lake before nightfall. US 2 was a four-lane highway at this point, and my chances of finding overnight accommodations seemed better along that route than on the back roads recommended by the Bikecentennial maps. I had left Minot without making plans for that night's lodging, so I decided to wait until I got closer to Devils Lake to find a telephone directory with listings for that town.

Making slow progress against the wind and the rain, by six o'clock I was still twenty-one miles short of my destination. At Church's Ferry I found a restaurant with a Devils Lake directory. I began calling parsonages, but there was no answer. After several tries, I realized the cause of my dilemma. This was Friday evening, and most people were probably gone for the evening. Cycling cross-country made me lose track of time.

I dialed one more number, and this time a pastor's wife answered. I made my customary appeal, confident of a place to stay. Thus far I was batting one thousand, for I had yet to experience a rejection on the trek; every previous request for lodging had met with success. But my fortune was about to change. The minister I had called was out on church-related business, and my request didn't strike his wife as being reasonable. A stormy night was not a good time for my first rejection.

Realizing my need to be resourceful, and recognizing an opportunity to exercise my "hopeful imagination," I asked, "Can you give me an idea whom I might call?"

"You might want to try the Law Enforcement Agency," she replied. "They take care of transients."

I wasn't quite sure how to take that suggestion. I certainly wasn't a transient, if by that she meant "vagabond" or "weirdo," although long-distance cyclists probably give that impression.

Seeing that the rain was turning into a downpour, I decided to pursue her suggestion. When I called the police station, I explained that I was cycling for Habitat, a cause strongly supported by former President Jimmy Carter, and that my attempts at finding lodging for the night had ended in futility. I was thrilled to hear the officer respond, sympathetically, "Come by our office when you arrive in Devils Lake. We'll have a place for you."

A couple of hours later I walked into the police station, where I was supplied with a meal voucher and a reservation for a motel room. I saw this as providential, for a motel room was just what I needed that night. It gave me a place to dry my soaked belongings and to enjoy some much-needed privacy. It had been a very long day; I had cycled well over one hundred miles, half of them in the rain.

Despite the soaking, I was jubilant as I spoke with Wayne that evening. Two days later he would provide an update on the trek to a crowd gathered at the community park in Washington for the third annual Gospel Music Rally. On that occasion our church would conduct a Sunday morning service in the park, followed by an afternoon and evening of musical entertainment, presented by local Christian artists. This year's donations were designated for Habitat. I was glad to supply Wayne with some good news to pass on. I wouldn't have been so positive a few days earlier.

That night we also finalized plans for our rendezvous in Fargo, plans that went back to that Sunday in July when I first announced my intention to cycle cross-country for Habitat. A member of our church had offered Wayne an airline ticket to meet me at the halfway point, and Fargo had seemed an ideal spot. However, when Wayne examined his calendar for the fourth week in August, he noticed he was scheduled to participate in a five-day leadership training event later that week in Washington, DC. That meant he had to travel to Fargo on Monday, August 21 and return on Wednesday, August 23. So the one item that never changed on my itinerary was the entry for Tuesday, August 22: "Fargo—DAY OFF!"

Stage 20 (August 19): Devils Lake to Cooperstown – 84 miles

Rain was in the forecast for Saturday morning, with heavy storms predicted for nearby Minnesota, so I was delighted to find the sun shining as I awakened. Before leaving town, there were chores to finish, including repacking all my stuff, spread across the motel room to dry. I also wished to send my daughter a birthday card, for I would miss her birthday for the first time. While enjoying my free breakfast, I inquired about the town and its unusual name.

Devils Lake is located in the midst of a lush lake region, once populated by Indians and wild game. It currently offers some of the best goose and duck hunting in the entire North and is still home to Indians, Sioux and Chippewa, who live within the Spirit Lake (Fort Totten) Reservation to the south.

The name "Devils Lake" goes back to the Sioux word *minnewaukan*, meaning "mystery" or "spirit water." Legends abound concerning this body of water, including accounts of mythical sea monsters and phantom ships, but one story with a probable historical basis relates how Sioux warriors attacked the Chippewa against the advice of a seer and were drowned in the lake by a storm as they returned from battle. The Indians named it "Bad Spirit Lake." When Christians populated the region, they simply took the name one step further and called it "Devils Lake."

That morning I found reason to be thankful for the previous day's rain, for the new weather pattern caused the wind to blow out of the northwest. The brisk breezes pushed me along Route 2 at a speed close to twenty miles an hour; on a loaded bike, that's moving!

As I pedaled across the eastern portion of the state, the words "amber waves of grain" from *America the Beautiful* came to mind. Everywhere I looked, golden fields of wheat stretched endlessly, verifying the state's claim as the nation's number one cash-grain state. Indeed, North Dakota is first in red spring wheat (used for baking flour), durum wheat (used for pasta), malting barley, flax, and rye.

As I cycled through North Dakota, the silence of my rhythmic pedaling was disrupted by a pinging sound, coming from the direction of my wheel spokes. But the sound was not mechanical. It came from grasshoppers, legions of them, warming themselves on the hot pavement. Every turn of the wheel resulted in a detonation, as bodies exploded like shrapnel. Their presence was a nuisance, to farmer and cyclist alike.

The terrain flattened as I approached the Red River Valley of the North. Riding along quiet roads provided me time to think, to recall conversations held along the way. The night before, for instance, had been "Ladies' Night Out" at the restaurant in Church's Ferry. There I met a group of ladies, mostly of retirement age, enjoying one another's company. Each had a story to tell, a question to ask, or some motherly advice to offer, such as why I shouldn't be riding a bicycle down the highway at night in the rain. Yet by the sparkle in their eyes, I could sense their overall support of my adventure.

Following that entertaining repartee, I met a Norwegian gentleman at the counter, who promptly continued where the ladies had left off. "How many nationalities do you think there are in North Dakota?" he asked. I was interrupted halfway through my list with the right answer, "Only two. Norwegians and those who wish they were." And that was the first of many jokes. The man had missed his calling as a stand-up comedian.

I reached Cooperstown shortly after five o'clock that Saturday evening. Though I had not yet made plans for the night's lodging, I wasn't overly concerned, for Cooperstown was renowned for hosting hundreds of cyclists during the annual American Lung Association Trek. I headed toward the local park, because that's where the cyclists camped during their stay. It was a good decision, for the entire town seemed to be gathered there. A celebration was in progress, with music and lots of food. I considered mingling with the crowd but then decided that my first priority should be to find the local Presbyterian church, which I knew to be nearby.

When I arrived at the church I was surprised to find the doors open with people coming and going. As the congregation was holding a farewell party for its pastor of eight years, I felt conspicuous in my tight-fitting cycling outfit, especially with everyone else dressed up. But I was invited to stay, and after a quick change into my "best" clothes, a pair of jogging pants and a clean Habitat T-shirt, I felt more presentable.

Hoping to blend in, I decided to introduce myself with a bit of humor, noting that I had cycled 1,600 miles to attend the reception. Some of the parishioners guessed I might be the pastor's brother, since both of us were tall and lanky. But one dear lady, speaking with utter sincerity, stole the show when she asked, "Are you our new pastor?" It was time to explain.

Earlier that day I had asked myself the question, "I wonder what surprise God has for me today." Each stage of the trek was teaching me to rely upon God's providential care, and I was discovering that as I put myself in positions of vulnerability, I was coming to expect the unexpected. However, the surprises awaiting me in Cooperstown pushed the limits of the unexpected to an extreme.

My immediate need was food, and plenty of it. I had not been able to find any restaurants or cafés along the back roads that day. Consequently I had missed lunch altogether and was famished. Fortunately, the farewell party involved a potluck supper, which meant that there was plenty to eat. The serving dishes were loaded with carbohydrates, ideal for a hungry cyclist.

During dinner I learned how the congregation became Presbyterian. I had noticed earlier that there were few Presbyterian churches in rural communities across the northern Plains. North Dakota was Lutheran country, aside from Catholic parishes and a sprinkling of Methodists and independent Baptists. So I wondered how this rural Presbyterian parish had come into existence. I was told that at one time there had been two congregations of separate denominations that wished to merge. But since neither denomination was willing to capitulate to the other, they compromised and joined a third denomination. Unlike many such unions, this merger really worked.

After supper the ladies loaded large zip-loc bags with chicken, pastries, and other goodies, providing more than I could carry. In addition to food, my other concern was for overnight housing. And that was provided by Janice Johnson, the hostess for the pastor's farewell reception. Her husband, Gary, had remained at home with Cody, their sick six-year-old son.

Though it wasn't exactly "Guess Who's Coming to Dinner?" the arrival of a stranger on a bicycle must have caught him by surprise.

The journey of faith is full of surprises, and cannot be undertaken without relinquishing self-sufficiency. But if we are willing to trust and take risks, as the apostle Paul stated in his letter to the Philippians, then we can claim the promise that "God will supply every need of [ours] according to his riches in glory in Christ Jesus" (4:19).

That night I had difficulty completing my stretching routine on the dining room floor, for Patch, their lovable mongrel, was eager to play. Though I could hardly concentrate as my face was licked clean, I felt like part of the family. The conversation that followed was meaningful and profound. Once again the way had been paved for instantaneous fellowship, the sort of camaraderie that accompanies membership in the "family of God."

Janice spoke about the joys of living in a small town in North Dakota, surrounded by hardworking and caring people in a state that boasts the lowest crime rate in the nation. But all was not perfect in Griggs County. Times had been tough since the Great Depression, reflected in a 46 percent drop in population since 1930. Economic woes impacted the families that remained, particularly those constituting the weakest link in the human chain: newborns and infants.

That evening Janice related a story of courage and faith, an account of her family's perseverance against overwhelming odds:

> Our daughter, Casey, was born on January 19, 1984, six weeks premature. She seemed perfect in every way. When she was four months old she caught a cold that wouldn't go away. We took her to Doctor Salmon, who gave her some medicine. Then soon after, on the night of Wednesday, June 6, my son Cody awoke at nine-thirty, kicking and screaming. My husband was not at home. I called friends to sit with Casey and to take Cody and me to the emergency room. It turned out Cody had a severe ear infection.
>
> At the same time I told Dr. Salmon that Casey had a red spot in her eye. He told me to bring her in the next day, instead of waiting until Friday for her regular appointment. This was the first of many "lucky" breaks. When the doctor saw her he thought she just didn't look "right," so he had a blood sample taken. When they poked her tiny toe, it bled profusely. I could tell when the doctor came back into the room that it wasn't good news, but I never thought it could be so bad. He thought she might have leukemia.

He had trouble calling the hospital in Fargo, as all medical facilities were bracing for a potential tornado. Shortly after five that evening we got the call from Dr. Salmon telling us to take Casey to Fargo as fast as possible. With her white blood count at 250,000 (normal is between 5,000 and 11,000), she could have a stroke at any moment and die. We took off immediately in a genuine North Dakota thunderstorm.

I am a strong advocate of infant car seats, but that night when Gary brought in the car seat for Casey, I refused to put her in it. I knew I had to hold her all the way to Fargo, for if she died, she had to be in my arms. We made it to Fargo, and what a helpless feeling I had when the nurse came and took our baby from my arms and whisked her off to the intensive care unit. When the doctor told us later that night that if she could make it through the next twenty-four hours maybe she would have a chance, all we could do was count the hours and the minutes. Gary's parents came from Valley City and sat with us that night.

I could not count the many prayers said that night for that little girl. We received a call in the intensive care unit from our pastor's wife. Our pastor was out of state, but she had started two prayer chains for Casey. We cried on the phone together. The staff let me feed Casey and hold her often that night. Each time we left her we had to wonder if it was the last time we'd see her alive. I was the one who had to call friends and relatives with reports. It's OK for the mom to cry, but hard for the dad. Once, however, I did catch Gary crying.

Casey did make it through those twenty-four hours, surprising the nurses and her doctor. After five more brushes with death, two and a half years of chemotherapy and many, many prayers, she has been pronounced cured from leukemia. We had to wait five years for that, but it was worth it. She appears normal in every way, but we continue to watch for any possible brain damage, as she was on an experimental treatment that could cause brain damage. There has been absolutely no sign of any brain damage, and it now seems unlikely that there ever will be. I could give you many examples of God's hand during her illness, but what I've told you is enough.

The local people rallied around Casey's need, providing meals for her family and then later, a benefit auction. A nearby county held another benefit and a local bank set up a fund to help pay for expenses. Janice concluded, "Without that extra help, I don't know how we'd have made it. Sure, in a small town everybody knows everybody else's business, but that's not always bad. It's an opportunity for people to help one another."[1]

It was that same spirit of mutual support and encouragement, of hospitality and generosity, which had made my trek possible. In the Plains States, America's heartland, times are tough, but faith is tougher still.

Stage 21 (August 20): Cooperstown to Fargo – 94 miles

I left the Johnson home that Sunday with a parting gift, the telephone number of Carolyn and Curtis Haugen, their relatives in Fargo. A telephone call the night before had gone unanswered, but I was assured they would take care of me. Fargo was ninety-four miles away, and I wasn't sure I could make it that far in one day. It depended on the wind. But I was one day ahead of schedule, so I could complete the trip in two days if necessary.

By one o'clock, however, I was halfway to Fargo. A tailwind, together with unusually cool temperatures in the high fifties, made for ideal going. A telephone call to the Haugens resulted in the promise of lodging for the night.

Several hours later I cycled into Fargo, on an access road that ran parallel to Interstate 29. As I neared the airport, I was greeted by a thunderous ovation as six military jets performed pinpoint maneuvers in formation across the clear North Dakota sky. The Air Force Thunderbirds were completing a dazzling performance at the air show, part of the state's centennial celebration. The aerial display became for me a victory celebration of sorts. I was halfway home; the toughest 1,700 miles lay behind me. The crowds lining the roads near the airport might have missed the triumphant look on my face, but Fargo represented the trek's midpoint, and I was entitled to some emotion.

Fargo had always been more than just another city in my mind. There was a special quality—something enigmatic and mystifying—that distinguished this place from others. John Steinbeck attested to it in his *Travels with Charley*: "Fargo to me is brother to the fabulous places of the earth, kin to those magically remote spots mentioned by Herodotus and Marco Polo and Mandeville. From my earliest memory, if it was a cold

---

1. A short while later, Casey was once again diagnosed with acute lymphomatic leukemia; chemotherapy treatments resumed. "We thought this nightmare was over," Janice wrote, plaintively.

day, Fargo was the coldest place on the continent. If heat was the subject, then at that time the papers listed Fargo as hotter than any place else, or wetter or drier or deeper in snow. That's my impression, anyway."[2]

My stay confirmed Fargo's reputation for extremes: constant winds (a study conducted over a year's period revealed only one calm day), severe storms, but also extraordinary hospitality.

That evening I spoke with Wayne by telephone. The Gospel Music Rally, just concluded, had been a great success, and he was preparing to fly to Fargo the following day. I had good news for him as well. The Haugens had invited him to join me at their home for the next two nights.

Carolyn and Curtis Haugen had worked hard to create a home full of love, for God as well as for one another. They had come to Fargo several years earlier from Griggs County, near Cooperstown, where they still owned a farm.

Earlier, while living on the farm, they had endured numerous trials and setbacks, including times of deep depression. Financially, they had come close to bankruptcy, and within their immediate family, one son had experienced a near-fatal accident when a farm tractor collapsed on him. Despite their adversity, or more accurately, *through* it, they discovered the calming power of prayer and the immediate presence of God. Praise, prayer, and the Scriptures had become stepping-stones in their walk with God.

As the Haugens shared their story of transformation from nominal Christians to confident believers, Carolyn concluded, "We called ourselves Christians all our lives, yet we had never really known the Lord or allowed God control of our lives. Since our spiritual renewal, despite problems and trials, we can certainly say we have never walked alone."

Stage 22 (August 21): Fargo – Making up Lost Mileage

The following day, invigorated by the friendship and testimony of these new friends, I set out for a day of cycling through the Red River Valley, intent on using this extra day to make up lost mileage.

The Red River of the North is one of the few major rivers in the world that flows in a northerly direction, emptying into Lake Winnipeg in Canada. Formed north of Lake Traverse, South Dakota, by the conflu-

---

2. Steinbeck's subtitle for his cross-country adventure is worth noting: *In Search of America* (New York: Viking, 1962), 121–122.

ence of the Bois de Sioux and the Otter Tail rivers, it flows north between North Dakota and Minnesota, forming the boundary between them. Most of its course runs through a level plain, one of the richest farming areas in the world. At one time a huge glacial lake, Lake Agassiz, covered much of North Dakota and Minnesota. As the lake retreated, around 6000 BC, it left behind the fertility of this great river valley.

My ride followed a rectangular pattern through western Minnesota. East of Moorhead the roads ran straight for miles, parallel to huge fields planted with sugar beets, sunflowers, potatoes, and wheat. The wind was blowing out of the southeast again, and I longed for the forests of Minnesota, farther to the east, where I knew I could count on at least partial wind cover.

That night the Haugens dropped me off at the airport around six o'clock, when Wayne was scheduled to arrive. A storm was brewing as I arrived at the airport, and I was relieved that Wayne's commuter plane landed just before the storm hit. I waited impatiently by the gate, having anticipated this moment for days. I watched the passengers disembark, but Wayne wasn't among them. When the last person had come down the ramp, I knew Wayne had missed the flight.

As the terminal emptied, I found myself walking alone through the small airport. I thought about my plans for the evening, including going out to eat and using Wayne's rental car for sightseeing. As I glanced in the direction of a car rental booth, an attendant waived me over and said, "Are you Bob Vande . . . ?" He couldn't quite pronounce my last name, but he had a message from Wayne. A delay in Pittsburgh had caused Wayne to miss his connecting flight in Minneapolis, but he would be on the next flight, due to arrive in about ninety minutes.

This news made me uneasy, for by now storms were blanketing the entire Fargo area. The shuttered sky turned black as wind and rain pounded angry rhythms against the terminal building. For two and a half hours the storm lashed out before succumbing to the promissory arc of a rainbow. Wayne's plane descended through that shaft of light and landed safely.

A short while later I saw Wayne's familiar figure pass through the gate. But he looked different. His face was ashen white and he looked badly shaken, although he smiled bravely as we embraced.

On the way to the restaurant Wayne told me about his connecting flight from Minneapolis. The plane had flown northward, towards Duluth, in an attempt to skirt the storm. But the wind turbulence eventually caught up to the plane, pitching it about like a toy. Seated next to Wayne was a young lady, obviously distraught. As the two of them bounced around in their seats, they knew they were in peril.

Attempting to disguise her fear, the young lady turned to Wayne and asked, "Is this the worst you've ever seen?"

Wayne countered, responding reassuringly, "No, I've seen worse." Of course, he was lying through his teeth. He had never experienced such turbulence. That night, a thirty-five-minute connecting flight had become a ninety-minute nightmare.

An hour later all was normal again as Wayne and I indulged in pasta at Valentino's, an Italian restaurant specializing in pizza. Besides the buffet, which included six varieties of pizza, there was a pasta salad bar, in addition to lasagna, conolli, and strawberry pizza for dessert. What a meal! This may have been the first time I had eaten more than Wayne at one sitting, though the rough airplane ride may have compromised his customary appetite. During the meal we contemplated the possibility of attracting a Valentino franchise to "Little" Washington, Pennsylvania.

Stage 23 (August 22): DAY OFF

The next morning we visited the Rev. William Bates, District Superintendent of the United Methodist Church in the Fargo area, hoping he might provide some prospects for lodging through Minnesota. Bob Armstrong, the Methodist minister from Pennsylvania, had already prepared the way with a telephone call, so Rev. Bates was expecting us. He suggested that we contact the Minneapolis office of the United Methodist Bishop, with its statewide connections, and that seemed like a promising possibility.

Following our visit, Wayne and I drove to Minnesota to look around, since we had free mileage with the auto rental. Two areas of interest were Detroit Lakes, the center of a resort region that contained some 500 lakes, and Tamarac National Wildlife Refuge, established in 1938 as a breeding ground for migratory waterfowl and other kinds of wildlife. We hoped to see some of the bald eagles that nest in the refuge.

Though we did not spot any bald eagles, Wayne noticed turtle trails running through the grassy waters of Tamarac's bogs, and that led to one of his famous stories about how he and his uncle used to hunt snapping turtles:

> As a child I remember seeing my uncles and older cousins come back to my grandparents' house on hot Sunday afternoons, after a day of hunting along creeks and ponds, and dump ten to twenty turtles in the yard. Years later, after I had been away from the area for twenty-five years, I reacquainted myself with old Uncle Boyd, and he and I began hunting snappers together. His method was simple, but quite dangerous. He would crawl along the bank of a stream or pond and stick his arm into the holes, pulling out turtles weighing up to twenty-five pounds, with heads the size of a coffee mug. Old Uncle Boyd had started hunting turtles when he was six years old. Over the years he had gotten his share of injuries, but he wasn't afraid of anything.
>
> His method was not for me. I trapped turtles by a process known as jugging. You simply fill a milk jug full of water, connect a steel wire about sixteen inches long to the handle, and attach a turtle hook on the end of the wire, using chicken parts for bait. Then you tie a rope to the handle and throw it in the water, securing the other end.
>
> There's a good reason why this works. Once the turtle grabs the bait it can't close its mouth enough to seal it. With its mouth partially open, it can't go under water for long or it will drown. Once a turtle has been hooked you can see the jug bobbing up and down, and you can pull it towards you.
>
> Of course you have to be very careful handling these snappers. They can jump, and their jaws are so powerful they can cause severe injuries, even biting off a finger. Using boots or heavy shoes, you roll them over and hold them down. Then you grab them by the tail, making sure to keep them at a safe distance. When it's time to kill them, I usually attach them to the limb of a tree with a long hook, and then I cut off their heads with pruning shears.

After Wayne finished his story, he clarified his reasons for hunting snapping turtles:

> Some people hunt them for sport, and that's certainly part of it. But I just don't like snappers. They are scavengers, who kill fish by taking out a bite and letting the rest go. They eat ducks, dogs, anything that gets within biting distance. They are mean and attack each other. A small child is not safe around the ponds or streams where they live.

Then he explained an important side benefit to hunting them:

> Turtle meat is considered a delicacy. And each turtle has seven different kinds of meat. For instance, the neck has a texture like lobster, while some parts of the leg are like the dark meat of a chicken and others more like beef or pork. The meat of the small turtles can be deep-fried, but you cook the large ones until the meat separates from the bones; then you cut them up and make turtle soup.

Wayne's entertaining stories were memorable and made for a relaxing day off. The day culminated with a visit to the Royal Fork Buffet restaurant. It was our turn to treat the Haugans, and at $5.35 for all you can eat, this was a meal we could afford. The buffet included five hot entrees, a salad bar, soups, vegetables, hot cinnamon rolls, beverages, a wide variety of cobblers and other desserts, and make-your-own sundaes.

On this occasion Wayne showed no restraint. Despite my hunger, I couldn't keep up with him or with Curtis Haugen, as their farmers' appetites left me in the dust. There would be no profit for the Royal Fork that night.

I couldn't have enjoyed a better thirty-six hours. Wayne's visit was just what I needed, and the Haugans, complete strangers only a few hours earlier, had been perfect hosts. The following morning we said our farewells and parted regretfully, Wayne to his leadership training conference, and I back to the trek.

Wayne offered to lighten my load by taking unnecessary items back with him. When I handed him a few small articles, he tested me: "Are you sure you don't want to give me your tent and sleeping bag?" As much as I wanted to travel lightly, I wasn't willing to part with items that might still prove indispensable. Too many uncertainties lay ahead.

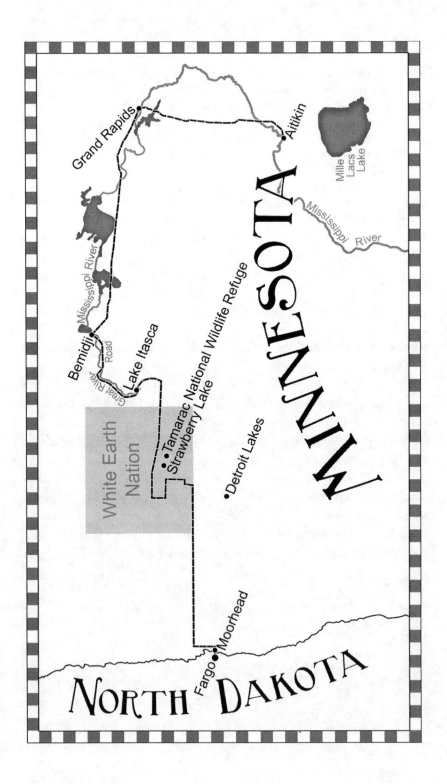

10

The Habitat Connection

STAGES 24–27: MINNESOTA— FARGO TO MILLE LACS LAKE [281 MILES]

Stage 24 (August 23): Fargo to White Earth Reservation – 67 miles

THE JOHNSON-HAUGEN CONNECTION, BEGUN in Cooperstown, North Dakota, yielded four days' lodging, and the network was expanding. Before leaving Fargo I was guaranteed a place to stay on my first night in Minnesota, with the Jacobsens. Roselyn and Talbert Jacobsen were related to the Haugens and lived in the small village of Strawberry Lake, sixty-seven miles from Fargo. This community, located within the White Earth Indian Reservation, was right on my route.

The wind continued to be an impediment as I pedaled the treeless stretches of western Minnesota. Most of the day, whenever I headed east, I fought a brisk crosswind. The topographical maps indicated flat farm-land, and that suggested easy cycling, but the bothersome wind blowing relentlessly across the open expanse was demoralizing. I longed for the shelter of Minnesota's famed woodland.

At Strawberry Lake, I located the dirt road to Roselyn and Talbert Jacobsen's trailer. Nestled along the southwestern side of the lake, the trailer and the handful of homes around it provided an idyllic setting. The remainder of the shoreline lay wooded and undeveloped, for it was part of the White Earth Indian Reservation. Some of the land had been sold to outsiders, but most of the lakeshore belonged to the Indians. At certain times of the year, non-Indian residents could hear Native Americans as they danced and celebrated festivities along the lake. Many of the non-native residents were concerned that the Indians, who had legal powers and complete charge of the reservation, might install gambling casinos nearby, as they had on other reservations.

Dinner that night included wild rice, purchased from the Chippewa Indians, who picked it from the nearby swamps, where it thrives. As we ate, our conversation naturally turned to the subject of Native Americans and the reservation system, a topic that came up regularly on my journey across the Northern Plains.

In those conversations, my hosts held out little hope for the future of the reservation system. Despite governmental aid in the form of free education, hospitalization, and low interest loans, widespread poverty and despair continue, with seemingly few Indians benefiting from the incentives. In the past, this predicament led many whites to conclude that assimilation and the abolition of reservations were the only solution.

Many Native Americans now desire to participate in the American economic dream, but they resent the dominant white culture and look instead for ways to maintain and preserve their own ethos. There is a growing consensus in America that agrees with that assessment, supporting the notion that economic improvement need not separate individuals from their natal group. Some years ago a wise observer anticipated the modern sentiment: "If every Indian who betters himself must become an 'ex-Indian' . . . then there is no way to reduce that group's poverty, short of its total elimination."[1]

Political squabbles, lack of shared power, social discrimination, and the continued restrictive nature of many governmental policies continue to plague the reservation system, even when Indians attempt to solve their own affairs. The "Indian problem" will not easily go away. And it will not go away by itself, for it is not solely an "Indian" problem; it is an issue that must be addressed by all Americans.

That night the Johnson-Haugen-Jacobsen connection provided me with the best accommodations to date, a guest cottage on one of the most peaceful of Minnesota's nearly 12,000 lakes.

The next day I participated in two birthday celebrations, one with my host, Tully Jacobsen, quietly enjoying another birthday in the autumn of his life, and one with my daughter Sara, celebrating her eleventh with relatives and friends back home in Little Washington. Congratulating Sara

1. Murray L. Wax, *Indian Americans: Unity and Diversity* (Englewood Cliffs, N.J.: Prentice-Hall, 1971), 195.

by telephone was actually quite difficult, for at that moment the distance between us seemed far greater than 1,500 miles. I felt guilty and homesick as I hung up the telephone, missing my family more than ever.

Stage 25 (August 24): White Earth Reservation to Bemidji – 86 miles

Today's journey was distinctive, for it included a visit to Lake Itasca, the source of the Mississippi River. From the start I had considered this land-mark as a high point of the trek; it was one of the reasons I had chosen the "northern tier" route.

The Jacobsens recommended travel to Itasca by an alternate route from the one suggested by the Bikecentennial map. Once again the wind was a determining factor, for it was gusting stronger than yesterday. Today's ride would be close to one hundred miles, and I wanted to spend as much time as possible enjoying Itasca before reaching Bemidji, my stop for the night.

Emotionally I was in high gear as I resumed my journey through White Earth Reservation. At Fargo I had taken Rev. Bates's suggestion and called Bishop Christopher's office in Minneapolis in an attempt to pin down overnight accommodations across Minnesota. That telephone call proved to be fortuitous, for it connected me to a statewide clergy network.

Stocked with a list of names and telephone numbers, I knew that this valuable resource was the product of my association with Habitat. In this state, as elsewhere along my route, I found United Methodists enthusias-tically supportive of Habitat's vision. Though the same was probably true of other denominations, in Minnesota the United Methodist denomina-tion became my supply line.

My first contact with this network, a call to the Methodist church in Bemidji, confirmed the commitment. De Pickett was the first to answer my appeal. Her congregation was in the midst of its annual rummage sale, sponsored by the youth group, and De, as coordinator of volunteers for the church, was in the thick of things. But she assured me that I could stay at the church: "We've got a hideaway bed you can use," she said, "if you don't mind the mess."

When I asked her if she had heard of Habitat for Humanity, she responded enthusiastically. As it turned out, she was a member of the newly formed board of Bemidji's Habitat. Because this group was still unaffiliated, no one back in Washington, Pennsylvania, had known of its existence. Even Habitat International failed to notify us of this Habitat groundswell in Bemidji.

The morning's ride along Route 113 was pleasant. The occasional traffic did little to disturb this scenic route as it weaved through pristine forests and along alluring lakes. At one point the gently rolling terrain modulated slightly upwards. A sign at the summit informed me that I was crossing the Laurentian Divide. Unlike the Continental Divide in Montana, which divides the continent east and west, this ridge separates the watersheds of the Gulf of Mexico from those of Hudson Bay.

This region is remarkable not only for its innumerable lakes but also for the curious names given to some of those bodies of water. Beyond the Divide, a lovely lake bore the puzzling name, Bad Medicine Lake. I was intrigued by the odd name, which the Indians used for an imaginary huge fish. Apparently the original Indian name for the lake had the three letters b-a-d in it, thereby determining its English derivative. I'm sure a study of lake names in Minnesota could result in a fascinating book.

My heartbeat quickened as I turned onto County Road 1 and entered Itasca State Park. The main road through the park was quite narrow as it threaded its way along the eastern rim of the lake, some fifty to one hundred feet above water level. I decided to ride the park's undulating bike path, partly to avoid vehicular congestion on the road but also to yield to my adolescent impulses as I negotiated sharp turns and unexpected descents with abandon. At the Park Headquarters I called De Pickett to inform her that I was behind schedule but that I still intended to arrive by five o'clock, about the time she would be leaving the church.

A park ranger addressed my curiosity about the origin and proper pronunciation of "Itasca" (pronounced eye-tasca). The Indians had called it Elk Lake, but a naturalist named Henry R. Schoolcraft, who participated in the expedition that discovered the headwaters of the Mississippi in 1832, renamed it Lake Itasca, a word formed by dropping the first and last syllables of the Latin words for "true source," *veritas caput*, or ver*Itas ca*Put.

I stayed on the bike path until it descended to the small creek that flowed northward from the lake. Children and grownups were frolicking in its waters, only twenty feet wide and a mere four inches deep. It took me less than one minute to cross the headwaters of the "mighty Mississippi" as it began its journey to the Gulf of Mexico, 2,552 miles away. The Chippewa had understood the significance of this great water-way, which they called the Mee-zee-see-bee, the "Father of Waters," for it drains water from points as distant as the Appalachians in the East and the Rockies in the West.

Leaving Itasca around three-thirty, I knew I would probably not make it to Bemidji by the five o'clock deadline. The twenty-nine-mile distance required taking a shortcut that included five miles of unpaved road (my cycling map used the more precise wording, "five miles of *dirt*"). I hoped it meant "*packed* dirt," for I needed to make good time along this stretch. The paved alternative of forty miles was no longer possible under the time constraints.

When I saw the "dirt" road, my heart sank. Instead of packed dirt, the surface consisted of gravel and crushed rock. Lacking a choice, I entered boldly. The first two miles were laborious. The back wheel, with its heavy load, dug two inches into the soft gravel, while the loose rock mocked my advance. Sudden stops, precipitated by the shifting sand and gravel, regularly threatened to throw me from the bicycle. Simply remaining up-right was a chore. Finally, aware that I simply could not continue riding so recklessly, I dismounted and began pushing the bicycle. The snail's pace heightened my anxiety about inconveniencing De with a late arrival.

At that moment a pickup pulled out of a clearing in the road, about a quarter of a mile ahead. It was heading in the direction I needed to go, but by the time I thought to get the driver's attention, he was already beyond hearing range. I calculated that at my pace I would arrive in Bemidji as much as two hours late. It would take me forty-five minutes to reach the paved road, and then I had at least an hour's ride into town after that.

A half-mile later I spotted a house, the only one along that unpaved stretch, and in the driveway was the pickup I had seen earlier. I decided to ask for assistance. But when I knocked on the door, the response nearly paralyzed me with fright. The door was practically ripped off its hinges by what sounded like a pack of wolves on the other side. A burly man came to the door, mercifully keeping the wild creatures at bay. He commanded the watchdogs—for that's what they had become—into a back room. One of the hounds, a surly German shepherd, had been abused as a pup, caus-ing it to become extremely protective of its attentive new master.

When I explained my need to get to Bemidji by five o'clock, the bearded woodsman responded curtly, "Good luck!" My first thought was, "I guess he won't be of any help." However, pursuing my hopeful imagination, I risked asking if he would consider taking me to the paved road ahead, adding, "Would you do it on behalf of Habitat?" I could have offered to pay him, but I didn't want to compromise my "faith journey" too quickly. I hadn't come this far to handle matters in a business-like manner.

He responded, "Sure, if you don't mind the grease, molasses, and whatever else is in the back of the truck." He had just finished setting a trap for bears, found commonly in that area. Suddenly I realized why there were no other houses along that deserted road. This was bear country!

As he drove to the main road and beyond, he explained that he was a baker by trade, but that he also set traps for sportsmen, who hunt bear with bows and arrows. The price for setting the trap depended upon the size of the catch.

During that brief ride we exchanged information: he, on luring bears and setting bait, and I, on providing better housing through Habitat. We parted friends, mutually enriched by our shared disclosure. A phone call from a nearby booth assured me that De would be waiting in Bemidji. As I rode toward town I remembered the comment by St. Paul in 1 Corinthians 15:32, informing his audience that he had fought with beasts in Ephesus. And I wondered just how close I might have come to a similar encounter.

Later that night I did some sightseeing in Bemidji, a city situated along one of Minnesota's most attractive lakes. I pedaled to scenic Diamond Point Park and then followed Paul Bunyan Drive to one of America's most photographed monuments, the colossal statues of Paul Bunyan and his Blue Ox, Babe.

At the monument, I relived the myth:

> Paul Bunyan, king of lumberjacks, was the greatest outdoorsman who ever lived. This legendary superman, hero of the early logging days, is said to have been born in Bemidji, on the site marked by his giant, eighteen-foot statue.
>
> Paul grew so fast that one week after he was born he had to wear his father's clothes. A lumber wagon drawn by a team of oxen was Paul's baby carriage, and by the time Paul was one year old his clothing was so large he had to use the wagon wheels for buttons. On his first birthday, Paul's father gave him a pet blue ox, named

Babe, which proved to grow as fast as the boy, reaching a size of seven axe handles between the eyes.

Paul and Babe made a team that was spectacular in action. Babe dragged the mighty water wagons that sprinkled logging roads and made them icy for gigantic loads of logs taken from the forests by Paul and his crew. Once, the water wagon sprang a leak, creating Lake Itasca; the overflow tricked down to New Orleans to form the Mississippi River. Everywhere the giant ox stepped a lake was formed, and the area around Bemidji is dotted with hundreds of these reminders of the giant lumberjack and his pet ox.

Paul wandered afar from Bemidji at times, and when his crew logged off North and South Dakota, there was a problem of what to do with the stumps. The problem was solved by making a two-ton maul, with which Paul beat the stumps down into the ground, and this is the reason why there are so few trees today in the Dakotas. When Babe died he was buried in South Dakota, his burial mound forming what is known as the Black Hills.

The rivalry between neighboring states came to light when one of my Minnesota hosts asked me to name North Dakota's state tree. I was stumped, for I had hardly seen any trees as I rode across that state; that should have given me a clue to the answer: "the telephone pole."

As I stood dwarfed beneath the statues of Paul and Babe, I found it easy to get caught up in the rich lore surrounding Minnesota's majestic North Woods, a lore created by hardy, persistent folk who, together with the state they created, are "larger than life."

The next morning I met a few of Minnesota's larger-than-life folks. De had arranged a breakfast with Anita Spangler, Beth Oja, and Al Bontrager, members of Habitat's newly formed board. An hour, carved out of busy schedules, sped by as we shared commonly held dreams. One member, already deeply committed to her local Habitat project, contributed $34 to the trek. This willingness to further stretch her commitment reminded me of the biblical maxim, "Cast your bread upon the waters, for you will find it after many days."

Stage 26 (August 25): Bemidji to Grand Rapids – 72 miles

Later that morning I bucked the wind yet again as I pedaled east on US 2, my route across much of the northern tier. My destination was the city of Grand Rapids, seventy-two miles away. In Minnesota, Route 2 was a link in the "Great River Road," a network of roads 3,000 miles in length that connects the Canadian border with the Gulf of Mexico. I crossed the Mississippi River twice that day as it meandered from lake to lake in the direction of Grand Rapids, where it bends southward and becomes navigable.

At lunch, as I was ordering food at the counter, two men entered the café and sat at a table. One of them, Lloyd Anderson, invited me to join them. As I answered his questions about the trek, I saw him pulling bills out of his wallet. I suggested that he put his money away and become a partner by writing a check in the amount of $34. He agreed, but only if he could also pay for my lunch. He gave me an offer I couldn't refuse.

Later that afternoon I overtook two cyclists riding from Washington to Maine. Nan and Lewis were between jobs, and they were using this trip to clear their heads as they prepared to move from Illinois to Colorado.

We had much to talk about. I had gone without cycling companion-ship for weeks, and like a famished traveler, I feasted from this sociable smorgasbord. Lewis related a peculiar incident from Itasca State Park, where he had met a cyclist biking across the country on a tight budget. The fellow had become so bored cycling alone that he conjured up reck-less stunts to alleviate his monotony. One stunt involved making peanut butter sandwiches, which meant he had to unzip a pannier, pull out bread, locate a knife, find the jar, take off the lid, spread the peanut butter on the bread, and put everything back—all while riding his bicycle!

He was making progress on his challenge until the uncooperative lid slid from his hands and rolled out of sight. He stopped, looked ev-erywhere, but couldn't find it. When he saw Lewis and Nan riding by he asked them the peculiar question, "You wouldn't happen to have an extra lid for a peanut butter jar, would you?" Nan looked at Lewis and they laughed out loud. It just happened that Nan had emptied a peanut butter jar several days earlier, and for some reason she had not discarded it.

After we had ridden together for a while, Lewis asked if I wanted to participate in an "Indian run." I wasn't sure what that meant, but soon I found myself in a familiar pace line that cyclists use, alternating the lead to create a windshield for the others. I was amazed at Nan's ability, not only to maintain a fast pace, but also to increase our speed, despite her fully loaded bike. She was a newcomer to cycling, but previous marathon running had helped her adjust quickly to the challenges of a new sport. We parted company at Grand Rapids, promising to write to one another.

The following Christmas they informed me that they had completed their cross-country crossing and had relocated successfully in Colorado.

This had been a special day for me, as I met and added new friends to a growing list from across the country. My hosts for the night, Rev. Richard and Nancy Massaro, were soon on that list. Dick, pastor of a local Presbyterian church, had agreed to host me when the Methodist pastor was unable to help.

I joined the Massaros for an evening of satirical theatre, performed at the high school by a troupe of improvisational actors from Minneapolis. After weeks of high visibility, of promoting the trek and Habitat, I welcomed the opportunity to relax in the obscurity of a darkened auditorium and be entertained.

The day came to a close in the Massaro living room as I listened to Dick's stories about canoeing through Boundary Waters Canoe Area, near the Canadian border. This 150-mile-long tract of land, the largest wilderness area east of the Rockies, has been described as "the greatest canoe and fishing area in the world." I hope Dick's standing invitation to a canoe outing is still in effect.

A phone call to Wayne, my last call for a week, yielded the name of a family with whom I could stay several nights later in Stillwater, near the twin cities of Minneapolis and St. Paul. During that visit I would meet the director of one of Habitat's most successful affiliates.

Stage 27 (August 26): Grand Rapids to Aitkin – 56 miles

When I awoke that Saturday, it was evident that the weather would play a significant role in today's ride. The rain clouds looked so threatening that the Massaros suggested I stay with them another day. I had not been able to complete a call to the Methodist parsonage in Aitkin, where I hoped to spend the night, so the invitation to take the day off was doubly attractive. But it wasn't raining yet, and since it was possible that the storm might pass quickly, I decided to take my chances on the road. In addition, the wind was blowing from the northwest, and I was heading south. I didn't want to miss an opportunity to ride with a tailwind.

Because of the threat of rain, I headed straight for Aitkin on US 169, avoiding the circuitous back roads along the Mississippi River suggested by the Bikecentennial map. Having no plans yet for that night's lodging, I thought, ambitiously, that I might possibly be able reach Mille Lacs Lake, for I knew that the following day's ride to Cambridge would be long.

The downpour arrived after I had traveled only three miles. I made a sudden detour into a modern, beautifully landscaped Lutheran church. When I introduced myself to the pastor I realized he had more on his agenda than putting the finishing touches on the next day's sermon. The church schedule that day included a wedding and picture-taking for the new church directory. Despite the pastor's busy agenda, he invited me to his study and took time to call a colleague in Aitkin, who told me he would arrange my night's stay. It pleased me to think I would be staying with a Lutheran family. My trip through Minnesota would not be complete without sampling Lutheran hospitality.

When I returned to the church lounge to wait out the storm, I felt conspicuous greeting well-dressed parishioners in my cycling gear. To make matters worse, the wedding party had arrived early to pose for pictures in the beautiful outdoor gardens. A horse-drawn carriage was waiting to take the couple for a ride prior to the ceremony. But the uncooperative weather changed all that. Today's congregants formed an unlikely mélange as parishioners, members of the wedding party, and a lone cyclist all tried to make the best of adverse circumstances.

The downpour continued unabated for four hours. Finally, with the wedding about to start, I felt it was time to leave. I packed my belongings into trash bags that I found in the church kitchen, pulling plastic bags over each pannier as well as over my shoes. Then I secured everything with twist ties. I wouldn't win a beauty contest, but I hoped to remain reasonably dry.

As I prepared to leave, I exchanged good wishes with the bride's father and we agreed that better weather was on the way. Before long the rains subsided to a drizzle, and within an hour the sun appeared.

In Aitkin, my stay with the Munnekes led to several surprises, for my hosts, Bob and Darlene, had invited others to join us that evening for dinner. Godfrey, a political refugee from Ghana, had been a guest of the Munnekes for several months. His application for asylum in the United States had been rejected, and Rev. Munneke was now assisting him with an application for refuge in Canada.[2] Godfrey hadn't seen his wife or children for three years, and that night he mentioned his grave concern over the uncertain future of his gifted twelve-year-old daughter, who spoke twelve languages.

The other dinner guest, Ellen, was a friend of the Munnekes from a previous pastorate. Known as "the saw lady," Ellen was a most unusual person. After the Munnekes first met her, she relocated to the Ozark Mountains of Arkansas. There she struggled to provide for herself and her daughter while making room in her heart for others. Eventually she went to Haiti as a volunteer in one of Mother Teresa's projects.

In Minnesota she supported herself by painting used saw blades; hence her nickname. She sold her artwork to passersby and at flea markets. Despite her meager circumstances, she was building a cabin with the assistance of a neighbor and friends from the church, but primarily with her own hands. She feared that carrying heavy stones might damage her hands and with them her livelihood.

My heart went out to this lady of unusual courage and faith, and I determined to see how Habitat might come to her aid. Her words to me across the table were unforgettable: "I *love* the poor," she affirmed, the emotion within her rising. Then she added, with even greater intensity, "I have a *passion* for the poor, and I have chosen a life of identity with them."

That night, as she was leaving, she pressed something into my hand. It was a $5 bill. I tried to refuse, knowing her impoverished condition, but she insisted, with a look of uncompromising determination, "Take it! And buy yourself a meal." I clutched this "widow's mite" for what it was, a priceless treasure.

2. Since then, Godfrey's application for political asylum in Canada was also turned down. I do not know what happened to him, though he decided to continue the appeals process in the United States.

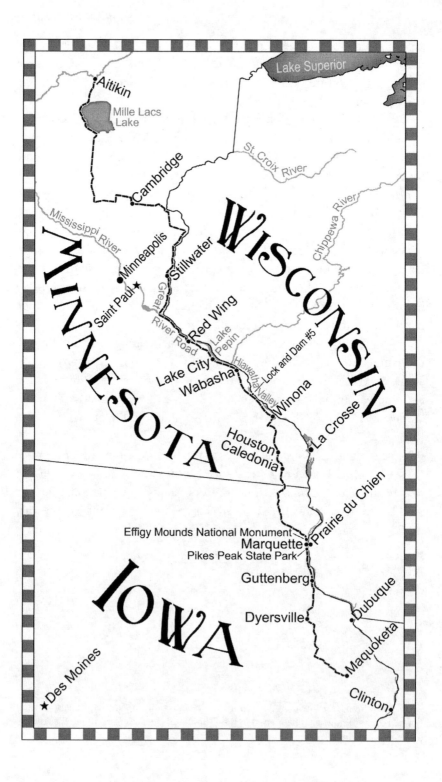

11

Along the Mississippi

STAGES 28–33: SOUTHERN MINNESOTA AND IOWA—MILLE
LACS LAKE TO CLINTON [442 MILES]

Stage 28 (August 27): Aitkin to Cambridge – 100 miles

SUNDAY MORNING I LEFT Aitkin early, aware that I had one hundred
miles of cycling ahead. It was a perfect day for biking: cool and sunny,
with a tailwind. Fourteen miles later I reached Mille Lacs Lake. As I gazed
at the lake, one of Minnesota's largest, its immensity beckoned me.

I walked along one of several piers that jutted into the lake, thinking
about the people I had met the previous night, then of others who had
helped shape my "Habitat connection." As the mosaic took shape, I recognized that my trip was more than a coincidence, more than an adventure;
it was part of a grand design. The trek represented my life, my pilgrimage
of faith, my calling as a Christian.

I tossed a pebble into the water, and as I watched the rippling effects
extend outward, I knew I should write this book. My story might inspire
others to understand their pilgrimage and to take greater risks of faith.

Spurred by a vision of expanding horizons, I sped southward along
the lake and Mille Lacs Indian Reservation. With the wind to my back,
I decided to remain on Rt. 169, ignoring less congested alternate routes.
After lunch I pursued my southerly course, anticipating a leisurely Sunday
afternoon ride. Little did I know that the next forty-five minutes would
provide the most frightening moment of the trek. The map indicated that
Route 169 turned into a four-lane highway south of the lake, with wide
shoulders. But the fifteen-mile stretch prior to that newer section was ex-

tremely narrow, with loose sand for a shoulder. As I proceeded along that section of the road, my only choice was to ride the narrow pavement.

To make matters worse, as the roadway narrowed, the flow of traffic increased. Suddenly I found myself caught up in a torrent of traffic. This bottleneck, built to the specifications of a bygone age, was not equipped to handle the waves of recreational vehicles, campers, boat trailers, vans, and trucks that surged forward at the rate of sixty miles per hour. I was unaware that on Sunday afternoons, especially during the summer months, this route functions as a major north-south artery, disgorging tens of thousands of weekenders on the Twin Cities, seventy-five miles away. If I had been traveling in an automobile, it would have been unnerving, but on a bicycle, it was insane.

I was too far along the route to turn back. My only choice was to pedal—and pray. I found myself pedaling over twenty-five miles per hour, as fast as my legs would turn, my prayers keeping pace. It was a bizarre cacophony: brakes squealing, horns honking, vehicles swerving, people shouting. Everyone seemed impatient, annoyed by the rainy weekend and anxious about the week ahead. For forty-five minutes this human tornado raged about me, drawing me into its vortex. It was the fastest fifteen miles—though it seemed the slowest—I had ever cycled.

When I reached the four-lane highway, conditions suddenly returned to normal: busy traffic moved in an orderly fashion as a cyclist pedaled calmly along a well-paved shoulder. But for one-half hour, on a Sunday afternoon in August, I felt I was in Pamplona, at the running of the bulls. I was fortunate to be alive.

Stage 29 (August 28): Cambridge to Stillwater – 66 miles

In Cambridge I stayed at the home of Harry Argetsinger, a pharmacist and avid cyclist who lived along the Bikecentennial bicycle route. When I arrived at the modern passive solar home, I was greeted by Judy and her younger son Paul, the latter sporting a T-shirt that posed a cyclist's dilemma: "In Minnesota there are two seasons: winter and road repair."

Later on I met Harry and his fourteen-year-old son, who had spent the afternoon completing a fifty-mile cycling workout. We spent an enjoyable evening talking shop as we compared cycling experiences and exchanged advice.

That night I called my wife in an official capacity, because for one week, while Wayne was away at a conference, she acted as my Habitat contact in Pennsylvania. Our conversation turned to the topic of overnight accommodations, always high on my list of priorities. The "Habitat Connection" had already arranged lodging for the next two nights, so we looked ahead to Lafayette, Indiana, where another Habitat affiliate was located. The director was a former cross-country cyclist, and I anticipated spending my final non-cycling day with him.

The following day I cycled into Stillwater, a historic river town located on the scenic St. Croix River, near Minnesota's Twin Cities. The region's commitment to bicycle safety was impressive, for a grid of designated bicycle routes spanned Washington County. I hoped that Washington County in Pennsylvania might follow suit.

Ann and Carroll Rock, my hosts in Stillwater, carefully planned my visit. We ate supper at a "pancake house," joined by several couples from First Presbyterian, the Rock's home church. My dinner companions had recently volunteered labor at Twin Cities Habitat, so they had lots to talk about. Steve Sydel, the newly appointed director of the organization, also joined us for the meal. This five-year-old affiliate, coordinated by Steve and his five-member staff, had grown dramatically during that brief span, expanding to four neighborhood chapters. I eagerly accepted Steve's invitation to join him the following morning in the Twin Cities for a tour of Habitat projects and to meet his staff.

After dinner, the Rocks suggested that we drive through Stillwater. From the bluffs overlooking the broad St. Croix River we admired the stunning view of the historic city below, nestled against the river's edge. Having served as a center for the logging industry in pioneer days, Stillwater hosted the Minnesota Territorial Convention in 1848. The following year Minnesota became a territory, and then, in 1858, a state. Stillwater, the first town site and county seat in the state, is appropriately called the birthplace of Minnesota.

Today this charming city of quaint shops, stately homes, grand hotels, and elegant restaurants, continues as a center of tourism, offering spectacular views of the "Rhine of America," as the St. Croix River is known. Portions of the river are preserved and protected for public use under the Wild and Scenic River System, administered by the National Park Service.

The following day I awoke at six o'clock and soon thereafter Carroll and I headed into Minneapolis together, he to work and I for a tour with Steve Sydel. The morning passed quickly as I visited several sites constructed or renovated by Habitat during the past two years, each one matching a family in need with a tailor-made miracle.

Most of these projects were the result of charitable contributions. Some homes were purchased for a single dollar; others had been donated and moved to empty lots. Steve indicated that one hospital both donated a house and paid part of the moving expenses, what it would have cost to tear the house down. Several local merchants had provided building supplies, including a manufacturer of prefabricated homes, whose donated materials for a new house were valued at $40,000. Built by Habitat volunteers, it became home to a single mother with six children, who were living in a shelter after the house they rented had been sold.

That morning I gathered valuable information on Habitat topics such as staffing, budgeting, recruiting volunteers, expanding neighborhood involvement, procuring properties, and raising endowment. My promotional visit ended with a tour of St. Paul, the state's capital, and a ride along the Mississippi River, which flows between the Twin Cities.

From Carroll Rock's office I telephoned Rev. Bob Armstrong to inform him of the changes in itinerary that Susan and I had discussed the previous night. Bob had been a big help in locating suitable overnight accommodations, but the itinerary he was using, with scheduled stops at campgrounds and other remote areas, was no longer valid. The past several weeks had been tough for Bob and his wife Maudie, due to the sudden death of their son, but my call found them eager to resume their involvement with the trek. Bob was confident that he could locate housing for the remainder of my journey

Stage 30 (August 29): Stillwater to Wabasha – 60 miles

It was almost noon when I concluded my tour of the Twin Cities with Steve. I was concerned about the late departure, because I still had a long day of biking before I reached Wabasha. Carroll agreed to transport me to the outskirts of St. Paul, where I could get a head start.

As I followed the Mississippi on its southeasterly course, I pedaled through Hiawatha Valley, called "one of America's most beautiful scenic drives." My ride included mandatory visits to shops in Red Wing (famous for pottery since the 1870s as well as for leather and shoe factories) and a stop at Lake City, known as the birthplace of water skiing. This resort town, called the "City of Parks," is located along Lake Pepin, a beautiful thirty-four-mile-long body of water formed by the merger of the Chippewa and Mississippi rivers.

Across from Lake City, near the town of Pepin, lies the birthplace of Laura Ingalls Wilder, author of the "Little House" books. An unfurnished log cabin, located in a beautiful park, simulates the one in which the Ingalls family lived.

Leaving Lake City, I asked a gas attendant the distance to Wabasha, and he responded, beaming with pride, "About fifteen *beautiful* miles." Years earlier Mark Twain also punctuated his description of the upper Mississippi with superlatives:

> The majestic bluffs that overlook the river, along through this region, charm one with the grace and variety of their forms, and the soft beauty of their adornment. The steep, verdant slope, whose base is at the water's edge, is topped by a lofty rampart of broken, turreted rocks, which are exquisitely rich and mellow in color—mainly dark browns and dull greens, but splashed with other tints. And then you have the shining river, winding here and there and yonder, its sweep interrupted at intervals by clusters of wooded islands threaded by silver channels; and you have glimpses of distant villages, asleep upon capes; and of stealthy rafts slipping along in the shade of the forest walls; and of white steamers vanishing around remote points. And it is all as tranquil and reposeful as dreamland, and has nothing this worldly about it—nothing to hang a fret or worry upon.[1]

Some features have changed, but much remains the same.

That night I stayed in Dorothy Fenton's home on the banks of the Mississippi River, six miles south of historic Wabasha. This town, one of the two oldest communities in the state, remains among the few true-to-life river towns. The elegant Delta Queen steamboat and its newer sister sternwheeler, the Mississippi Queen, make scheduled stops at Wabasha on their frequent excursions to St. Paul from St. Louis. The downtown business district, nominated for placement on the National Register of Historic Places, is like a page from Sinclair Lewis's *Main Street*. It includes

---

1. *Life on the Mississippi*, (New York: P. F. Collier, 1917), 338.

the Anderson House, Minnesota's oldest operating hotel, serving customers since statehood in 1858.

Wabasha is on the edge of the Upper Mississippi River National Wildlife and Fish Refuge, an area that extends southward for 261 miles to Rock Island, Illinois. Encompassing 155,000 acres of wooded islands, marshes, sloughs, and backwaters, this preserve was the first refuge in the United States to include fur-bearing animals, fish, and plant life. Lakes formed by spring floods make this one of the greatest breeding grounds for small-mouth bass. Dorothy loved the wildlife and actively fed an extensive population. Her yard, high on the riverbank, seemed an extension of the refuge as squirrels, wood ducks, geese, pelicans, and swans came to feed.

Dorothy's love of nature was matched by her love for people. Living with her were her ninety-seven-year-old mother and her brother-in-law. As we talked, I heard stories of the many individuals whose lives she affected. I learned about Pam, a former neighbor who was currently cycling around the United States, stopping to help people in need or for work when money got low. I also heard about children from an unchurched family who had enrolled in a church confirmation class due to Dorothy's persistence, even when others had given up on them.

One story involved her pastor, Rev. Dennis. Once, during a church service, a parishioner asked him to pray for the family of a young girl who had died recently by falling from a moving vehicle. This was the first Dennis had heard of her death, and he was so emotionally distraught that he couldn't continue with the service. Seeing his condition, Dorothy prayed quietly for him. As she prayed, she noticed an immediate change in his demeanor, and he resumed the service with a powerful extemporaneous prayer and sermon. At the conclusion of the service Rev. Dennis thanked Dorothy, adding: "I knew you were praying for me. I felt your strength."

Dorothy invited several guests for dinner that night, including her beloved Rev. Dennis. It was a joy to meet him in person and to exchange inspirational stories. The feast that followed included my first sampling of the Midwest's famous sweet corn.

The following day Dorothy packed a huge gourmet lunch, so large I could hardly carry it on my loaded bicycle. Later, her letter captured my sentiments exactly: "Your visit was like that of a lost friend who had just come home for a few hours." By now it had become quite evident to me that mentioning America's magnificent bounty required paying tribute to its greatest resource: her people.

Stage 31 (August 30): Wabasha to Caledonia – 71 miles

I continued south along the "Great River Road," stopping at Lock and Dam #5 to examine the network that keeps river traffic moving smoothly along America's greatest waterway. Operated by the Army Corps of Engineers, the lock is run by eleven employees, with two on the "wall" at all times. Twenty-nine locks and dams, built during the 1930s to control commercial navigation and to prevent flooding, are in place between Minneapolis and St. Louis.

Though the river can be navigated at night, thanks to the marked channels one thousand feet wide and nine feet deep, the upper Mississippi is navigable only eight months out of the year, on account of the thick ice buildup during the winter months. Barges account for much of the traffic along this section of the river. Individual tugboats push up to fifteen barges, three wide, with each barge carrying up to one hundred railroad cars of coal or grain. Unfortunately, no traffic was "locking through" at the time, so I visited the observation platform, where a tape recording provided additional information.

I followed the river to Winona, enjoying the delightful ride. At Winona I left the river road and pedaled along the steep bluffs toward Caledonia, my last stop in Minnesota. A two-mile climb brought me to the top of the ridge. I rode parallel to Interstate 90, then underneath it, recalling that four weeks earlier I had driven across that very overpass in the Little House. The nostalgia provided some perspective, for I was now over two-thirds of the way home, having completed 2,350 miles.

In Houston, at an attractive town park, I unpacked Dorothy's lunch with care, preparing for a leisurely meal. But as soon as I spread the food on a picnic table, swarms of yellow jackets appeared. The garbage cans had recently been sprayed and my unwelcome guests were irritated by their sudden food shortage. Their presence ruined my meal and I had no choice but to move on.

I arrived in Caledonia at two-thirty, my earliest arrival yet. My hosts, June and Marvin Wiegrefe, were exemplary. Though retired, both tackled a common problem for senior citizens in rural America, the lack of public transportation. Marvin regularly drove elderly patients to a medical facility in LaCrosse, Wisconsin, twenty-five miles away.

It was evident that the Wiegrefes were held in high esteem by their neighbors. Shortly after my arrival, Nathan stopped by. He regularly visited Marvin, but today he was eager to discuss my bike trip. It was a joy to help this precocious six-year-old anticipate the day when he could discard his training wheels and go forth to conquer the world.

After dinner Marvin introduced me to Ron, a retired social worker who had coped courageously with multiple sclerosis. When Ron asked me to explain the concept behind Habitat, he thrilled to the idea of people helping people in need. June Wiegrefe put her own volunteering experiences into perspective when she added, "Retired people need to remain active and useful. We feel good about helping others. It takes lots of people working together to make a good community."

June and Marvin reminisced about a trip ten years earlier as they steamed up the Mississippi from St. Louis to St. Paul aboard the luxurious Mississippi Queen. They remembered sitting in the paddleboat's lounge at night, listening to a Dixieland Jazz band play carefree tunes and watching the crowds gather along the banks to gaze at the elegant vessel as it paddled upriver. This steamboat experience allows modern passengers to recapture the excitement, the pampering, and the nostalgia of a bygone era, once a way of life along the Mississippi.

During my stay with the Wiegrefes I leafed through a copy of Peter and Barbara Jenkins's autobiographical book, *The Road Unseen*. Peter's earlier book, *A Walk Across America*, had inspired my own cross-country trek, and I read with pleasure their insights on other adventures.

Stage 32 (August 31): Caledonia to Guttenberg – 78 miles

The skies looked ominous as I headed toward Guttenberg, Iowa. Despite the threat of rain, I had to keep pedaling, for my itinerary through Iowa and Illinois was in place. The Methodist bishop's office in Minneapolis had provided a list of churches to call regarding lodging in Iowa. In Pennsylvania, Bob Armstrong was making additional arrangements, so accommodations for the remainder of the trip seemed promising. It was nice to be rid of this worrisome concern; the down side was that I had to stay on schedule.

Envisioning my ride through Iowa, I had expected nothing but flat roads and cornfields. The sign at the state line read "Welcome to the Heartland," and the cornfields on both sides of the road heightened my expectations. But my hopes for easy riding in Iowa proved illusory. Northeastern Iowa turned out to be a continuation of the Mississippi bluffs.

In addition to the hilly terrain, a headwind blew stiffly from the south. About mid-morning a cold, steady rain began to fall.

As I descended a long grade along the Mississippi, my eye caught a sign, partially blurred by the falling rain. Backtracking, I read the words "Effigy Mounds National Monument." Although I had no idea what this meant, I couldn't resist the possibility of warmth and shelter.

Paying the entrance fee, I headed for the restroom to dry off and change my wet socks. In the museum I learned that the region's prehistoric Indian burial mounds, built in the shapes of birds and other animals, are unique to the high bluffs and lowlands of the Upper Mississippi River Valley. Of the 191 known mounds within the monument's boundaries, 29 are in the form of bear and bird effigies. Some of the mounds are huge; the Great Bear Mound, for example, measures 70 feet wide, 137 feet long, and 3½ feet high.

During a lull in the storm, I continued along the river to Marquette, named for the French explorer Father Jacques Marquette. In 1673, this Jesuit missionary traveled down the Wisconsin River by canoe with Louis Jolliet in search of the Mississippi River. These two became the first known white men to set foot on Iowa soil.

The twenty-mile ride from Marquette to Guttenberg was no ordinary ride. Cycling the bluffs is a challenging and unforgettable experience because one moment you're in a valley, the next moment on top of the world. Beyond Marquette the road climbs two miles to Pikes' Peak State Park. The park, downriver from historic Prairie du Chien, Wisconsin, provides a spectacular view of the Wisconsin River as it merges with the Mississippi far below.

Later, as I labored up yet another hill, a car approached from the rear. The driver motioned me over and I recognized him from the overlook at Pikes' Peak. He had pursued me to make a monetary contribution to Habitat. Unsolicited donations, no matter the size, buoyed my spirits and confirmed my sense of mission.

When I arrived in Guttenberg, I was soaked, as were my belongings. Like attending physicians in an ER, Jim and Shirley Rozendaal came to my rescue. My shoes and raingear were placed next to the hot water heater, and a small fan was added to expedite drying. Shirley washed and dried my clothes and tried her best to sew my rotting leather biking gloves, now practically useless. That night a powerful lightning storm moved across the Mississippi Valley, dumping up to eight inches of rain. On nights like this I was grateful not to be camping in a tent.

After dinner I was treated to a Dutch Reformed custom, a reading from the Psalter Hymnal, followed by a devotional reading. The devotional selection told of a lone hiker in Arizona who, while running out of water, was limited to an occasional sip. The author suggested that in their walk through life religious pilgrims should thirst after righteousness and drink freely from God's unending flow, instead of limiting their spiritual intake to irregular drops. Though this insight applies to everyone, it seemed appropriate to my situation.

Jim had been a pastor in the Reformed Church prior to becoming a United Methodist minister. In the hallway of his home hung a picture of his graduating class from Western Theological Seminary in Holland, Michigan, an institution that his father-in-law served as president. He pointed out a famous classmate, Arie R. Brouwer, formerly General Secretary of the National Council of Churches. This family's ecumenical spirit was embodied by Jim's wife Shirley, a student in the divinity program at the Presbyterian Seminary in Dubuque.

Shirley spoke of the growth of Habitat in Iowa, mentioning how the twelve United Methodist District Superintendents had agreed to dispense with their customary retreat later that year in order to spend a week working on a Habitat project. Leaders are supposed to set an example, and theirs was a compelling model.

The Rozendaals responded enthusiastically to my curiosity about the area. They were proud of their town, for the entire downtown was listed in the National Historical Register. Guttenberg, settled by Germans in 1845, was named for Johanes Gutenberg (1397–1468), the inventor of movable type, who printed 210 Bibles from 1452 to 1455. Thirty of these had been printed on vellum or sheepskin, provided by 5,000 sheep. A replica of a Gutenberg Bible was on display in the *Guttenberg Press* office, one of 310 Bibles copied in 1913 from an original.

Anyone cycling in Iowa eventually runs across RAGBRAI, the world's largest and oldest bicycle touring event. The acronym stands for the Registrar's Annual Great Bike Ride Across Iowa, an annual ride sponsored by the *Des Moines Register*. The organizers go to great lengths to insure that a rider represents each state. The event is always held during July, "when the corn is high enough to insure privacy for those necessary stops," Jim Rozendaal explained. And that explanation makes a lot of sense. How else do you handle the needs of up to 10,000 cyclists when nature calls?

Iowa native John Boyer wrote a jingle in the 1980s to celebrate the annual event. The song was sent to every radio station along the previous year's 479-mile trek. The lyrics go like this:

> Honey, pack up my tent and my bicycle shoes,
> This is the main event, no time to lose.
> Gotta change the tires, oil up the chain,
> My soul is on fire, here we go again.
> Bikin' cross Iowa! Bikin' cross Iowa!
> While ridin' bikes across I-O-W-A!
> On the RAGBRAI Special, comin' your way!

Though RAGBRAI is a sporting event, it is also a great social event. Couples have met and married on the RAGBRAI Special. The route varies from year to year, but one tradition remains the same: placing one's back wheel in the Missouri River at the start, and the front wheel in the Mississippi at the finish. Some people go to extremes at the grand finale, when they throw their bicycle and their belongings into the river.

The following morning Jim took me to the nearby Kann Manufacturing Company, maker of linear aluminum recumbent bicycles. The manufacturer provided us with test models. After a brief adjustment period I found these extraordinary bicycles to be both comfortable and effortless to pedal. A prototype had been developed in the 1920s and 1930s, but the bicycles were banned from most races because their high efficiency gave them an unfair advantage. It felt weird riding mod-looking contraptions down streets named Mozart, Haydn, and Goethe.

Stage 33 (September 1): Guttenberg to Maquoketa – 67 miles

Leaving Guttenberg for Maquoketa, my second and final stop in Iowa, I climbed several steep bluffs before arriving at a plateau. Aided by a tailwind, I quickly came to the town of Dyersville, with its imposing basilica. German Catholics had settled many of the towns along today's route. Every town had a cathedral, its steeple visible, like a beacon, for miles.

In Dyersville I visited the imposing Basilica of St. Francis Xavier, surmounted by twin spires, 212 feet high. Completed in 1889, this minor basilica was one of only thirty-three in the United States at the time. Known as the "prairie basilica," it is the only one in the world located outside an urban area.

The term "basilica" comes from the Greek word *basileus*, meaning royal or kingly. Unlike a cathedral, which is a bishop's or archbishop's church, a basilica is the pope's church. This particular church was declared a basilica in 1956 by papal edict for its unusual architecture and on account of the parish's spiritual vitality.

My departure from Dyersville followed the same route used only a few weeks earlier by some 8,000 RAGBRAI cyclists. I wondered what it might be like to ride in such a sea of bicycles. For a day or two it might be fun, but I preferred solitude to a throng.

Later in the day I noticed a sign on a farmhouse lawn that read, "Keep America Strong—Stop Trade with Communist Countries." The message seemed anachronistic in 1989, when sweeping changes were bringing the Cold War and communism to an end in Eastern Europe.

My host that night, Rev. Duane Manning, a retired minister, had asked that I telephone from Maquoketa when I arrived in town, since the directions to his farm were complicated. He suggested that we meet at the local United Methodist Church and that he would take me to his home from there. However, as I approached Maquoketa, I felt I might be passing near his house, so I looked for a way to spare both of us the extra miles. I stopped at a farmhouse a few miles from town and dialed Duane's number. But the line was busy. I continued on to Maquoketa, where, after forty-five minutes of trying unsuccessfully, I finally found someone who knew the directions to their house.

Orpha and Duane Manning lived at the end of a two-mile stretch of unpaved road, and their house was not easy to find. My unannounced arrival caught them by surprise, for they were expecting my call. After introductions, I asked whether a telephone had inadvertently been left off the hook. The Mannings were a bit embarrassed to find that that was the case.

This family was profoundly committed to a natural lifestyle. Living on a 130-acre farm, free of pesticides and herbicides, they raised their own wheat and ground their own flour and corn, from which they made corn meal. Several family members lived on the farm, including their son and daughter-in-law, who lived in a modified-berm passive solar home they had built by themselves. The Mannings practiced what they preached, improving the environment through healthy choices.

The next morning I found a cup of hot coffee awaiting me at breakfast. Since the Mannings were drinking coffee, I joined them, just to be sociable. At the conclusion of the meal, when the conversation turned to the subject of coffee, I confessed that I no longer drank coffee regularly, having broken the habit some years earlier. The Mannings admitted they didn't drink coffee either, but had served it out of politeness. We were amused by our strict etiquette, misguided though politically correct.

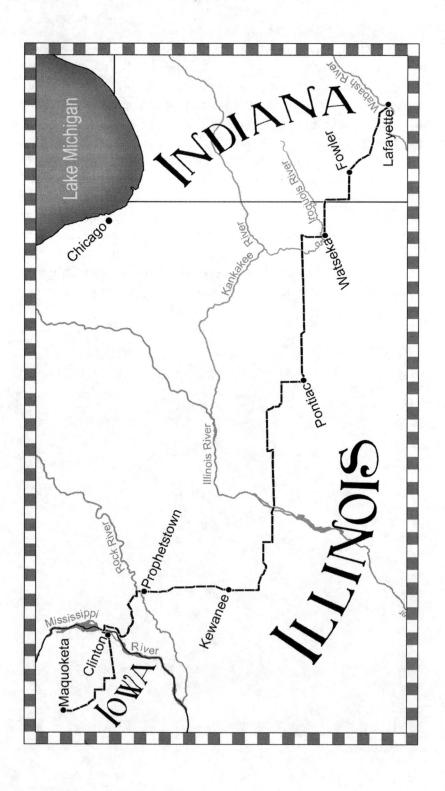

12

Excess Baggage

STAGES 34–38: ILLINOIS AND INDIANA—
MAQUOKETA TO LAFAYETTE [331 MILES]

Stage 34 (September 2): Maquoketa to Kewanee – 109 miles

I LEFT MAQUOKETA WITH great expectations. Today I would cross the
Mississippi River and head due east, straight for home. But the day's
ride would not be easy. Besides heading into a rogue wind, I encountered
lengthy detours, including a fifteen-mile stretch on US 30. This dangerous
truck route had no shoulders, so I was forced to compete with truckers,
notorious for their dislike of cyclists. Fortunately today was Saturday, so
traffic was lighter than usual. As I neared the Mississippi, the highway
narrowed, making cycling impossible. Another detour through the city of
Clinton led me to the North Bridge, where I finally made the crossing.

On the pedestrian walkway I paused for one final look at the magnificent river. The Mississippi, North America's greatest river highway,
seemed more than a river. For over a century it had borne much of the
nation's commerce on its broad shoulders and since my departure from
Itasca ten days earlier, it had provided me faithful companionship. It was
time to bid farewell to another newfound friend.

Today's century ride was physically and emotionally draining. On a
bicycle, morale is as vital as liquid, and the wind can have a searing effect.
Nothing is more demoralizing to a cyclist than pedaling across flat terrain in low gear. Traffic, road surface, detours, flats, breakdowns, weather,
terrain—all affect a cyclist's mood, but none is more debilitating than an
unfavorable wind, particularly during solo rides.

Cyclists counter the mood-altering effect of these factors with morale boosters: intriguing ideas, pleasant memories, snatches of conversations, even unusual landmarks—anything to break the monotony or help maintain the pace. Traversing the Cascades, climbing the Rockies, crossing the Mississippi, each success had provided a vital psychological boost.

Notwithstanding earlier success, as I pedaled toward Kewanee into a headwind I "hit a wall." Despite making physical progress, inwardly I felt defeated. Reflecting on my frustration, I concluded that feelings of powerlessness need not control our attitude. We can quit—and fail—or we can change our attitude about life's adversities, befriending them, if possible, or at least embracing them as mentors. Wisely, I chose the latter option.

I arrived in Kewanee, Illinois, late that evening, fatigued but 109 miles closer to my destination. Kewanee, the self-proclaimed "Hog Capital of the World," was celebrating the thirty-sixth annual Hog Capital of the World Festival. Had I arrived earlier, I could have enjoyed a day at the races—hog races, that is. Other activities that day included the hog day stampede (a four-mile run), the hog day antique car show, the hog day parade and carnival, a hog calling contest, and of course, the "world's largest pork chop barbecue." This town, literally, had gone "hog wild."

That night Harry and Edna Prince were my hosts. Harry, a retired minister, worked part-time on the staff of a large, local congregation. The Princes had volunteered to be my hosts, not only because I represented Habitat, but also because they had heard I was a professor at Washington and Jefferson College. They used to live near Pittsburgh and their son had attended summer school at W & J.

Edna took one look at my emaciated physique and made it her job to feed me. I had been burning around 800 calories *an hour* as I cycled across the country, and this high metabolic rate had left me fifteen pounds underweight; my face told the tale. In Kewanee, I attempted to regain some of that weight by eating "like a hog." Later on Edna reflected on the situation when she wrote: "It was hard to visualize the appetite and thirst you would bring with you, but luckily we fixed twice as much as we would normally have eaten, and with additional ice cream and cookies in the evening, I do believe you might have been filled."

During my brief stay with the Princes, I was impressed by their ability to empathize with my needs. Some people are gifted with an extraordinary hospitality, displaying it in such measure and with such grace that it surpasses a purely human quality. This "gift of hospitality," one of many spiritual gifts mentioned in the New Testament, is described as lavish, meaning that it is boundless and unrestrained. According to Romans 12:8, lavishness typifies all spiritual gifts: "he who contributes, in liberality; he who gives aid, with zeal; he who does acts of mercy, with cheerfulness." The following verse, 12:9, summarizes the Bible's teaching about spiritual gifts with the injunction, "Let love be genuine"; Eugene Peterson's translation is equally compelling: "Love from the center of who you are; don't fake it" (*The Message*).

For the Princes, generosity was not a duty; it was a passion. Their home epitomized sacred space, an environment where the "still small voice" of God is heard loud and clear.

My observation earlier in the day about befriending my foes led to an additional insight. For some time I had been carrying unnecessary baggage. I had suppressed the urge to ship it home, for I was convinced that upon crossing the Mississippi River I would benefit from the prevailing westerly winds and the additional weight would become negligible. But that was not the case. With only an occasional interlude, the wind continued blowing in my face, as in the Northern Plains, and the open farmland provided meager shelter.

At this point in the trek overnight accommodations were practically guaranteed, and it seemed foolish to carry a tent, sleeping bag, pad, and ground cloth—twenty pounds of needless weight. Sunday morning, while Harry was at church preparing for an early service, I shared with Edna an inclination to send my excess baggage home. Without a moment's hesitation, she offered to pack and ship any nonessential items. That was the impetus I needed. Within minutes the bicycle was freed of considerable weight, more than I had imagined, for my excess baggage filled two large boxes. How absurd to have carried a tent for thirty-five days and 2,600 miles and never to have used it!

That experience yielded additional lessons. What needless gear was I carrying on my self-sufficient journey through life? If my calling as a Christian was to a life of pilgrimage, living simply in reliance upon God's ability to supply my deeper needs, what excess baggage had I been carrying for the past forty-five years?

Stage 35 (September 3): Kewanee to Pontiac – 103 miles

The following day, my second successive century into the wind, provided me with the opportunity to reflect further upon the events of the previous day. Realizing that I was still carrying excess emotional baggage, I began unpacking once again, this time identifying and discarding impediments such as anger, resentment, and spiritual pride. Like that snapped seat bolt in Sandpoint, Idaho, self-reliance and cherished emotional crutches only support so much weight before they crack. I resolved to seek out a support group upon my return home, replacing fragile psychological bolts with stronger spiritual ones. Eliminating autonomy, independence, and other self-sufficient patterns would free me for greater service and usefulness. The wind and my excess baggage became powerful metaphors of grace, mentors to lighten my load through the Trek of Life.[1]

At that moment of insight, an amazing thing happened. The wind changed directions, and for the next forty-five minutes I enjoyed a tailwind. Even though it reverted to a headwind, the tailwind became a metaphor of what Marcus Borg calls a "thin place."[2]

As I approached Pontiac, my thoughts turned to the original inhabitants of this land, their presence so indelibly preserved in place names across the state of Illinois. The region I had cycled the previous day, between the Mississippi and Rock rivers, was once one of the most concentrated wildlife habitats in the central part of North America, and it was this abundance of wild game and fur bearing animals that originally made this area so attractive to the Indians. Following the tragic end of the Illini on "Starved Rock," outsiders entered this region, including the Sauk from the Green Bay area of Wisconsin and the Winnebago, also from Wisconsin. This latter tribe established a village at what is now Prophetstown, on the south bank of the Rock River.

When I passed through Prophetstown two days earlier, I had inquired about its unusual name, expecting some connection with the Bible

1. I appreciate the encouragement I receive from my wife Susan, who regularly reminds me that I returned from this trip a changed person.

2. Building on an insight from Celtic spirituality, Borg explains that the metaphor is lodged in a perspective that affirms at least two dimensions to reality: the visible world of our ordinary experience as well as the sacred, understood not only as the source of everything but also as a presence that interpenetrates all things. "In 'thin places' the boundary between the two levels becomes soft and permeable, the veil becomes diaphanous and sometimes lifts"; see Marcus J. Borg and N. T. Wright, *The Meaning of Jesus* (New York: HarperSanFrancisco, 1999), 250.

or possibly with Joseph Smith, founder of the Mormon Church. I was surprised to learn that the town had been named for Chief White Cloud, called "Prophet" by the Indians because of his prediction that the white settlers would soon expel the natives.

The white settlers, particularly the farmers, discovered the land's true wealth in the deep black soil. And it was farmers, working that rich glaciated soil, who laid the groundwork for today's billion dollar corn crops.

Today the area between the Mississippi and Illinois rivers, known as the Corn and Hog Belt of America, consists mostly of grain-livestock farms. Nowhere else in the world is so much grain fed to animals. The land east of the Illinois River, however, is one of the most productive cash-grain regions in the world, with corn, soybeans, and oats the principal crops.

In Pontiac I stayed with the Kidds, who housed me in their luxurious guest quarters, complete with private bath. This professional couple, Don a printer and Pam a gynecologist, lived with their daughter Jessica and their three dogs on the outskirts of town. The kitchen belonged to members of the family *and* to the three dogs, but not to guests or intruders. Ted, the most ferocious canine, let me know who was boss. As soon as he saw me, he sprang across the room and lunged against the Dutch door separating us, barking wildly. I drew back, fearful for my life. That meager barrier kept the trek alive.

Stage 36 (September 4 – Labor Day): Pontiac to Watseka – 58 miles

Labor Day dawned cool and bright. Following an interview with a newspaper reporter, one of about a dozen throughout the trek, I left for Watseka, near the Indiana border, only fifty-eight miles away. Continuous crosswinds added a challenge to the straight, checkerboard-style roads that characterized this flat farmland.

Boredom was a factor to contend with on days such as this. Like the weary cyclist in Minnesota who spread peanut butter sandwiches while riding, I too searched for distractions. At times I contented myself with trivial pursuits, noting that 270 pedal revolutions constitute a mile at sustained speeds of fifteen miles an hour. Singing, reciting Scripture, praying for others, meditating on the lessons of nature, and other devotional pursuits also proved beneficial.

My attention eventually shifted to my homecoming, six days later. Wayne indicated that he had scheduled a reception for two o'clock on Sunday, September 10. Invitations had been sent to former President Jimmy Carter, to the County Commissioners, and to the mayor of Washington. Members of the media, supporters of Habitat, friends, and my immediate family would all be there.

I received that news with mixed feelings. My eagerness to rejoin loved ones was offset by anxiety over the distance yet ahead. Could I reach Washington in time? Though I was currently three days ahead of my original schedule, I would have to gain two additional days in order to reach Washington by the new arrival date. Good weather and favorable winds were essential.

That afternoon, as I neared Watseka on a two-lane road, a foolish prank by a carload of youngsters nearly caused a fatal accident. In the distance I noticed two cars coming toward me. As they drew near, the second car suddenly swerved to pass, accelerating rapidly as it came. Instinctively, I moved to my right, onto the road's shoulder. The passengers appeared to be teenagers, out for a thrill. As the car approached, the driver seemed intent on a game of intimidation. At the last minute, however, he did something foolish. Instead of pulling back into his lane, he veered further to his left, crossing the white line onto the shoulder. This was no longer a game; the car was heading directly toward me. To avoid a head-on collision, I ditched the bike. The car whizzed by, spraying gravel and debris everywhere. For some time I sat on the ground, dazed, thinking how close I had come to being a Labor Day statistic!

I reached Watseka around mid-afternoon, with visions of picnics and poolside parties dancing in my head. Because this was a holiday weekend, I decided to arrive as early as possible. Stopping at the home of John and Lori Rodda, I was surprised to find no one home. I checked the address again to make sure this was the right place. I tried the front door, then the side door, but both were locked. Hearing a dog barking inside, I thought of Ted, the Pontiac beast, and decided to remain outdoors. Finally, after a nap and some stretching, I entered the garage. The house was somewhat secluded and I needed evidence that this was the right house. Finding the door between the garage and the house unlocked, I opened it slowly, looking for signs of the dog. Seeing none, I entered the kitchen, and there, on a side table, was a letter addressed to the Roddas. That brought some relief, for at least now I wouldn't be arrested for illegal entry. I searched for some indication that the Roddas were expecting me, but my examination proved futile. Feeling uneasy about waiting indoors uninvited, I turned to go back outside. At that moment the garage door opened and Mrs. Rodda drove in with her two young children.

Lori mentioned that her husband John was at the local golf club competing in a tournament. His team was participating in a playoff. The uncertainty of my arrival time, coupled with the high drama of the match, led to the confusion. We returned to the golf course to watch the playoffs. I welcomed a change from my routine and was delighted to spend a few moments riding the fairways in a self-propelled golf cart. That night I slept on a waterbed. Going "Homeless for Habitat" had its advantages.

The next morning John invited me to ride his Pinarello racing bicycle. He often started the day with a training ride, but that day he had to get to work early, so he encouraged me to give his bike a try. Riding the Pinarello brought some discomfort, for the frame was six inches smaller than mine. In addition, riding this high-tech bike required wearing cleated shoes, and John's were two and a half sizes too small. The exhilarating ride, however, offset the inconvenience.

It took a few minutes to adjust to the feel of this state-of-the-art bicycle, with its indexed shifting and clipless pedals. The bike provided quick response and great acceleration, but the awkwardness of riding such an ill-suited vehicle cut short my trial run. The brief ride ended in humiliation, however, for when I came to a stop next to the Roddas garage, I attempted to dismount in the normal manner, by removing my shoe from the toeclip and extending my foot to the ground. Forgetting that my feet were locked into the pedals and unable to recover in time, I watched helplessly as the bicycle began its precarious lean, taking me with it to the ground. What an embarrassment! I was fortunate to land in the tall grass unscathed; more importantly, there were no spectators.

Stage 37 (September 5): Watseka to Lafayette – 61 miles

My morale was high as I headed for Lafayette, Indiana. There I would stay with another cyclist, visiting Habitat projects while enjoying my third and final free day of the trek. I hadn't taken a day off since Fargo, North Dakota, two weeks earlier.

As I rode to the Indiana state line, on secondary roads recommended by John Rodda, the state maps I carried proved useless. These were the most deserted back roads I had ever ridden. Everywhere I looked I saw nothing but corn, towering over my head. At times the road narrowed to an eight-foot strip of concrete as cornstalks crowded the pavement. I felt trapped by this eerie setting, alone in a world of corn.

At the Fowler, Indiana, town park, a librarian I met on lunch break informed me that Labor Day celebrations were a big thing in the Midwest. That made sense, since I had heard about the Kewanee hog festival and Pontiac's annual national harvesters' festival. She told me about the celebration in Earl Park, a small community north of Fowler, where 130 residents spent a full year planning for their Labor Day festival. Visitors can stay in a beautiful park, with space for trailers and tents and amenities such as built-in showers, all free of charge. That year's four-day festival had included a flea market with 135 booths, sporting events, tractor and truck pulls, music, food, and much more.

Civic pride—Midwesterners flaunt it.

Stage 38 (September 6): DAY OFF

I spent two nights in the Taylors's air-conditioned den in Lafayette, Indiana. When Wayne Armstrong had first contacted Habitat affiliates about my trip, my projected route skirted Lafayette by twenty-five miles. Doug Taylor, director of the local affiliate, responded eagerly to the trek, insisting that I spend a night at his house on my way through Indiana, even if that required a drive on his part to get me. Doug's enthusiasm led me to alter my route, and I cycled directly to Lafayette.

My arrival in Lafayette coincided with final preparations for Lafayette Habitat's fifth anniversary. During that period, the affiliate had completed eight projects, six of them new constructions. But this weeklong celebration, scheduled to begin in ten days, would focus on the future. Significant events included a "house blitz" (a Habitat term for building a house in a short span of time); a fifteen-kilometer Hike for Homes, connecting all eight Habitat houses plus current building sites; and an evening with David Rowe, president of Habitat for Humanity International. The emphasis was on deeds, not words, following the biblical admonition: "If anyone has material possessions and sees his brother in need but has no pity on him, how can the love of God be in him? Dear children, let us not love with words or tongue but with actions and in truth" (1 John 3:17–18, NIV).

That evening I accompanied Doug to a church meeting, where members of the congregation gathered to discuss deeper commitment to Habitat. Doug suggested various levels of involvement:

1. congregations can *adopt* a house, assisting in its construction;

2. congregations can *sponsor* a house, financing its construction; and

3. congregations can *commit* their volunteers to a particular skill (such as hanging drywall, painting, siding, framing, roofing, etc.).

Lafayette's Habitat had identified twenty-two specific tasks within the total construction process. Each task had a coordinator, and each coordinator worked with volunteers. As Executive Director, Doug supervised the coordinators and purchased all materials.

Doug spoke of commitment to specific tasks. "Habitat needs more than volunteer laborers," he said. "Individuals are needed to serve on committees, including Family Selection, Nurture, Worship, Site Selection, Building, Publicity, Volunteers, Coordination, and Hospitality."

As I contemplated the organizational profile of a Habitat affiliate, I remembered the words of Jim Tyree two months earlier, at my first Habitat meeting: "Plan for the future. Be concerned with the long haul. Habitat . . . must not collapse locally for lack of planning, prayer, or training." I thought of the Habitat leaders I had met along the trek, all competent, resourceful, energetic, enthusiastic, and visionary. I felt honored to be in such company.

I listened with interest as Doug explained the "sweat equity" expectations set by Lafayette's Habitat for client families: "Potential clients must complete one hundred hours of volunteer work on a previous home before they are selected as partners. Once selected, two hundred hours are required per adult member on his or her own home. Finally, when the home has been completed, clients lease the house for one year before they can purchase it." During this period, called the "Partnership Year," issues such as adequate maintenance and promptness in payment are addressed.

Once a family has completed the partnership year, its needs are not ignored. The nurturing and supportive process continues. A Home Owners' Association provides training in vital areas such as management of household and financial resources. This association, run by the partners themselves, creates bonds and deepens the sense of community among clients. As part of that process, each family is assigned an advocate.

"Partnership, not Patronage" is one of Habitat's mottos, which Lafayette's affiliate exemplified notably.

The following day I visited Doug and some volunteers as they prepared the foundation of the "blitz house." Previously, Doug had included various local unions in Habitat projects, and on this occasion, members of the local masons' union had constructed the basement walls. The "blitz house" would be built upon a solid foundation.

Doug explained that most of the Lafayette projects were new constructions because in that area it was difficult to find old homes available for rehabilitation. Proximity to Purdue University meant that landlords were always looking for old houses to repair as rentals to students.

Later, while joining Doug on some errands, I noticed a plaque on the wall of a local electrical firm, inscribed as follows:

> Habitat for Humanity gratefully acknowledges the volunteer spirit of _____.

> Your skills and time have helped us provide decent housing for God's people in need.

The plaque included a reference to Isaiah 58:12:

> And your ancient ruins shall be rebuilt;
> you shall raise up the foundations of many generations;
> you shall be called the repairer of the breach,
> the restorer of streets to dwell in.

An ecumenical ministry, with a global vision, involving total community resources, in partnership with low-income families: that's Habitat for Humanity!

Jimmy Carter once summed up the philosophy of Habitat like this: "What the poor need is not charity but capital, not case-workers but co-workers. And what the rich need is a wise, honorable, and enjoyable way of diverting themselves of some of their overabundance."[3]

Getting rid of excess baggage; that's a start.

During our second evening together, after the other members of his family had gone to bed, Doug and I swapped biking stories. Doug took out his cycling journal and began to reminisce about his cross-country

3. *Everything to Gain*, 105.

trips. While in high school he had organized his own tour, signed up ten friends, and with the help of a teacher, who followed in a support vehicle, cycled from Los Angeles to the state of Maine. Together they had designed and built a special trailer, which they later sold to a cycling organization. Several years later Doug interrupted his college studies to pedal cross-country once again, this time accompanied by a brother and a third companion.

The trials of my own transcontinental crossing clearly before me, I couldn't envision more than one such journey; but cyclists are known for their short memories. Exchanging anecdotes and acknowledging difficulties energized us for the tasks ahead: Doug for Lafayette Habitat's anniversary celebration and me for the final push home.

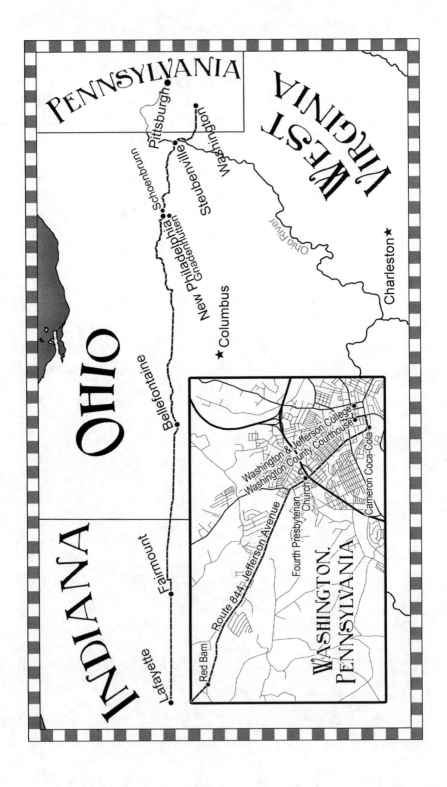

13

The Center of the Universe

STAGES 39–42: INDIANA, OHIO, WEST VIRGINIA, AND
WESTERN PENNSYLVANIA [406 MILES]

Stage 39 (September 7): Lafayette to Upland – 78 miles

THE FOLLOWING DAY I called Pete Povich at WJPA, Washington,
Pennsylvania's radio station. I wanted to provide his audience with
an update on the trek and also to invite listeners to my homecoming celebration four days later. In turn, I accepted Pete's invitation for an appearance on a subsequent Friday Pie Day Show.

Today's ride on State Route 26 was delightful, about as flat a ride as
any I had experienced on the trek, and certainly the straightest. But the
best part was the direction of the wind. Blowing out of the southwest, the
gentle breeze continued from that direction for the remainder of the trek.
I found my long-awaited tailwind.

Murphy's Law, however, was still in effect,[1] at least if Fairmount's
town bully had anything to say about it. Cruising through town in his di-
lapidated pickup, he approached me from behind, revving his engine. The
cacophony continued with a horn solo, blasting at close range. Unable to
perturb me, he modulated into a higher key. Stepping on the accelerator,
he shot past me, only to jam on his brakes after cutting directly in front
of me. Wary of his threatening behavior, I kept my distance, avoiding the
intended collision. At this point his engine stalled and he sat there in the
middle of the road, pathetically blocking traffic.

---

1. This "law," widely subscribed, contains the famous axiom, "If anything can go wrong,
it will go wrong"; its corollary, "Murphy was an optimist," is even more pessimistic.

Fairmount is famous as the native home of James Dean, the late movie actor. In September the town would host the fourteenth annual "Museum Days/Remembering James Dean" festival. Explaining that James Dean had been dead for some time, the waitress of a local restaurant expressed her dismay at the hype: "That's the problem. Some people here want to keep him alive. Like Elvis; he's alive somewhere, you know."

That night I stayed in the small town of Upland, Indiana, at the headquarters of the nation's premiere Christian cycling organization, Wandering Wheels. I had heard many stories about "Wheels," especially concerning "Coach" Bob Davenport, its founder and director.

Full of anticipation, I arrived at the Wandering Wheels office in Upland around mid-afternoon. Coach Davenport was most gracious in his welcome. Apologizing for his busy schedule, he explained that he was about to embark on an outing with military personnel.

"Under normal circumstances," he said, "I would wine and dine you," meaning he would provide me with first class accommodations at the Kitchen-Retreat Center across the street. He had only recently known of my coming and the retreat center was full, yet he still managed to make room for me in the staff building.

Meeting Coach Davenport, a legend in cycling circles, was a thrill. While in college, he had earned all-American honors playing football on a championship UCLA team. Following a career in professional football, he had accepted the position of head football coach at Taylor University in Upland. After eleven years of successful coaching, during which time he earned the permanent title of "Coach," he established Wandering Wheels around three stated purposes: "to ride a bike across America, to grow up in God, and to give away God."

It didn't take long to feel I had known Coach all my life. His disarming approach quickly cut through formalities. Despite his busy schedule, he gave me a tour of the center and drew me into a stimulating conversation on topics such as social awareness, the nature of Christianity, and biblical inspiration. There was no limit to his generosity as he gave me a free T-shirt, a complimentary book on Wandering Wheels (*Coast to Coast*), and then loaned me his own sleeping bag for the night. Surely this man's cup was running over.

Coach's ventures up to that point included two 10,000-mile "circle America" trips, which granted college credit to participants; two treks through China; thirty-three coast-to-coast tours; and a trans-America trip in 1988 for thirty cyclists from China. The visit by the Chinese was not repeated in the summer of 1989, partly due to the Chinese government's forceful response to a series of prodemocracy demonstrations led by students, intellectuals, and other activists between April 15 and June 4 of that year. The demonstrations, violently quelled by the ruling Chinese government at Tiananmen Square on June 4, led to an uncertain climate in China. Conservatives within the Chinese Communist Party attempted to curtail some of the free market reforms being undertaken as part of Chinese economic reform, but those reactions ultimately failed in the early 1990s, as a result of the collapse of the Soviet Union. Those events and the current climate in China temporarily stalled Coach Davenport's efforts to continue sponsoring such trips.

In addition to a full schedule of touring and cycling activity, Wandering Wheels has since acquired a 440-acre campground site in the Upper Peninsula of Michigan that offers a wide array of recreational activities for family vacations.

Coach talked about current hopes, including collecting sturdy old Schwinn bicycles for use by impoverished Mexicans and finding ways to respond to the needs of young people in troubled areas of the world who long for the American way of life. For a few moments I was captivated by Coach's exuberance, and then, like a whirlwind, he was gone. I cannot forget this visionary man and his bold, creative, ministry. His approach to life is well summarized by the following quotation, cited in *Coast to Coast*: "To travel, watch the darkness fall, arrive in a village, see the first lamps lighted and have nothing to eat, nor anywhere to sleep, and to let everything depend on God's grace and the goodness of men—this, I think, is one of the greatest and purest joys in the world."[2]

Stage 40 (September 8): Upland to Bellefontaine – 103 miles

I crossed into Ohio buoyed by a tailwind. The landscape was dotted with small towns, each only a few miles apart, their names revealing the German origins of the first settlers: Minster (named for Münster), New Bremen, Maria Stein, and farther north, Leipsic and New Bavaria. In the 1830s and 1840s German Catholics had come to Cincinnati, where they

---

2. Barbara Stedman, (Nappanee, Indiana: Evangel, 1988), 85, quoting from Nikos Kazantzakis, *The Last Temptation of Christ*, translated by P. A. Bien, (New York: Simon and Schuster, 1960), 235.

received one-square-mile plots on which to build towns. Today, some of these towns remain in such proximity that from one spot five cathedrals can be seen, each in a different town.

About twenty miles from Bellefontaine I stopped at a house to inquire about a shortcut into town. The lady mentioned some back roads I could take, and then she recommended that I stop at a nearby house and ask for a cyclist named Steve, who might want to escort me into town. When I remounted the bike, its response felt sluggish. Upon checking the rear tire, I found a slow air leak, caused, no doubt, by a small, sharp stone I had struck before stopping to ask for directions. This flat, the first and only one of the trek, ended an amazing record.

After repairing the tire, I continued to Steve's house. This teenager, an accomplished cyclist, had completed a 900-mile ride earlier that summer, traveling from Ohio to North Carolina with a group of Christian youth. He was making plans for the following summer, when he would participate in a ride across the country. The message on his T-shirt, "Love God, Hate Sin," declared the seriousness of his faith.

A delightful choice awaited me at the home of Butch and Sue Crawfis in Bellefontaine (pronounced Belle Fountain): dinner at the country club or charcoal-broiled steak at home. I chose the steak, and did not regret it.

Later that evening I placed a final phone call to Wayne. From the trek's inception, his encouragement had been remarkable, and even now he was working to make my homecoming memorable. Something about his name, Armstrong, reminded me of Peter, the disciple of Jesus whose name signified the reliability of a "rock." The world had been transformed once before by a handful of disciples, and it could happen again. I thought of my supporters—family members, Habitat partners, the Fourth Family—upholding me faithfully with prayers, assistance, and concern. In less than forty-eight hours I would rejoin them.

In the company of the Crawfises and several of their friends, I traced my route through an atlas, elaborating on the highlights of the trek. My hosts reciprocated with stories about Bellefontaine. Located on a watershed one mile from the highest point in Ohio, the town got its name, "beautiful fountain," from the natural springs at the site. I also learned that the first concrete pavement in the country was laid here in 1892, on the street surrounding the courthouse. The evening went by quickly until I glanced at my watch and saw that it was twelve-thirty. I excused myself, for a few hours later I would depart for New Philadelphia, a long distance away.

Stage 41 (September 9): Bellefontaine to New Philadelphia – 135 miles

Saturday's ride was magnificent. I was on familiar terrain now, practically in my own back yard. I had cycled across the state of Ohio several years earlier, on a marked bicycle route called the Cardinal Trail, and this morning's ride followed some of the same roads.

Ever since Lafayette, Indiana, I had experienced favorable winds, and this timely blessing, together with a reduced load, helped me average seventeen miles an hour. Reaching Washington by the following afternoon became increasingly realizable as the day progressed. By one-thirty I had reached Mount Vernon, two-thirds of the way to New Philadelphia.

The farther east I traveled, however, the hillier became the terrain. In Holmes County I passed farmlands belonging to the Amish and Mennonites, and towns named Millersburg, Walnut Creek, and Sugarcreek, catering to tourists through quaint shops and chalet-like restaurants. It was charming to see the horse-drawn carriages, driven by descendants of the "Pennsylvania Dutch" who settled here in large numbers as early as 1816.

New Philadelphia, Ohio, served as the final overnight stop of the trek. Joseph Taylor, my host for the night, was a music director in a local church. After his return from a singing engagement, we talked about his involvement with "Trumpet in the Land," a musical drama held nightly during the summer months in a nearby outdoor amphitheater. The drama reenacts the founding of Ohio's first settlement, Schoenbrunn, by the Reverend David Zeisberger in 1772. Surrounded by a band of converted Delaware Indians, Zeisberger and a group of Moravian missionaries built the first church and schoolhouse west of the Allegheny Mountains. The village served as a buffer between the British fort at Detroit and the colonists in the East. During the Revolutionary War, the suspicious British took Zeisberger, a pacifist, to Fort Detroit.

Shortly after the founding of Schoenbrunn, a group of Christian Indians traveled south to establish the village of Gnadenhutten, meaning "tents of grace." There, in 1782, these peaceful Indians were falsely charged with raiding, and all ninety-six were massacred by a punitive expedition of white militiamen under an American captain. The founding of this early settlement ended on a tragic note.

The drama's title, "Trumpet in the Land," was taken from a name given to Zeisberger, the missionary who courageously heralded the good news of the gospel. The title proved ironic, for the coming of the white man ultimately heralded bad news for the natives.

Stage 42 (September 10): New Philadelphia to Washington, Pennsylvania – 90 miles

I arose early on Sunday, September 10, eager to end the mad dash that had characterized the final days of the trek. It was drizzling as I left New Philadelphia, but my thoughts were hopeful and positive. The rough times, now behind me, had enlarged my spiritual horizons. I had met unforgettable people, enjoyed incredible scenery, and invested more deeply in Habitat. And now, as I completed the journey, the people, the landscape, and this commitment would be with me forever.

After crossing the Ohio River at Steubenville, then the Panhandle of West Virginia, I finally reached the border of Pennsylvania. This was the home stretch. I had chosen the final span into Washington deliberately, a serene ten-mile ride along a meandering creek known as Brush Run. This stretch, practically devoid of traffic, had always been a favorite place to bike.

As I neared the familiar red barn on Route 844, my rendezvous point with Wayne and others who agreed to provide an escort into town, a surge of emotion, like an electrical current, welled within me. Only six miles separated me from my goal, from family and friends.

As I made the final turn to the red barn, I reined in my emotions, not knowing what to expect. I was surprised to see only an old pickup, parked in the shade, its driver half asleep. Was this it, my homecoming reception? Had I arrived early or was I late? The awkward moment was dispelled as five cyclists dashed over the knoll of a nearby hill, whooping and hollering as they prepared to escort me into town. Then Wayne drove up and I found myself enveloped in a bear hug. I finally met my grizzly!

Soon friends from the church drove up, using two-way radios to communicate with folks at the courthouse. The man in the pickup stirred and took on a more official demeanor, as he was there to provide police escort. By 1:45 p.m. the caravan to the courthouse assembled and headed into town. Balloons, banners, and festive signs marked the way. The officer stopped traffic at major intersections and soon a long line of cars formed behind us. I paused at the Fourth Presbyterian Church, where friends had gathered to offer their congratulations prior to the formal ceremony. My pent-up emotions were ready to burst.

A mile later I rounded the corner to Main Street and commenced my final ascent, a gradual climb to the courthouse. At the top of the hill a sign stretched chest-high across the road, marking the finish line. The marker read, "We love you, Rev. Bob." I broke the tape at 2:01 p.m. A crowd of well-wishers surrounded me, and I knew my journey was over.

On the platform, Susan and Sara awaited me. Peter, competing in a soccer match, would join us later. The reunion was glorious.

Gary Nicholls, President of Habitat for Humanity of Washington County, began the ceremony by presenting me with two plaques, one from the local Habitat organization and another with a message from Millard Fuller, founder of Habitat. In addition, I received a plaque from the mayor of the city of Washington, on behalf of the Washington County Commissioners.

Then the Reverend Bob Armstrong delivered a brief message, informing the audience that I had just completed 3,401 miles, cycling cross-country for Habitat. That mileage appeared prominently in the following day's newspaper headlines. The program included several musical numbers, among them a duet rendition of Andrae Crouch's hymn of praise titled "My Tribute." Feelings of gratitude welled deep within me as I pondered the hymn's rhetorical question: "How can I say thanks for the things You have done for me?[3]

Finally, it was my turn to speak. Starting at the beginning, I described how an ordinary bicycle trip had become a trek. As I recalled some of the highlights of my adventure, I alluded to signage located at the entrance of towns announcing distinctive features of the community or notable accomplishments by its citizens. I remembered one sign in particular at the outskirts of a small town in Indiana that read: "The Center of the Universe."

"Right now," I concluded, "Washington is the center of the universe, for I am back, and this is home."

---

3. Bud John Songs (administered by EMI CMG Publishing, 1973).

Dr. Robert Vande Kappelle arrives at the finish line in front of the Washington County Courthouse. (Photo taken by Christie Campbell; courtesy of Observer Publishing Company, Washington, Pennsylvania)

Epilogue

WHEN I REACHED WASHINGTON, I still had mileage to make up, stretches when I had been unable to ride my bike. A couple of days after my return I cycled an additional 150 miles, exceeding my 3,400-mile goal. But I still had something to prove. Almost 400 miles remained to the Atlantic Ocean, and I wanted to complete my transcontinental ride, at least figuratively. I cycled those miles as well.

During the months of October and November I left home again, this time on a fifty-seven-day sabbatical trip to Europe and the Middle East. In addition to visiting archaeological and historical sites in eleven countries, I also cycled in three continents, beginning with the Netherlands, the land of my ancestors, where cycling is a passion.[1]

As the trek concluded, total paid-up pledges and other contributions neared $10,000, significantly higher than our initial expectation, but well below $34,000. The value of the trip, however, could not be measured in dollars and cents. I was pleased to learn that this $10,000 had included hundreds of contributors, with over eighty persons contributing the partnership sum of $34.00. That's the Habitat concept: a small amount can go a long way. That money made possible the construction of Washington County's first Habitat for Humanity house.

There is no way to estimate the impact a trip like this can have on the hearts and minds of people, not only in Washington County, Pennsylvania, but across our nation and world. Like that invisible mountain—that persistent headwind in the plains—Habitat volunteers will not quit until the vision is realized, until all who dream of a better future reach their destination. That invisible mountain must be crossed as well.

---

1. That account is told in *Into Thin Places: One Man's Search for the Center* (publication forthcoming). For a statement on the role of cycling in the Netherlands, see the essay on road cycling in the appendix.

Afterword: In Memoriam

Delbert Wayne Armstrong (1939-2010)

*Wayne's death was, for me,
the most profound religious experience of my life.*

—Peggy Armstrong

THIS BOOK IS DEDICATED to the life and memory of an uncommon individual. Wayne Armstrong transformed a cross-country cycling adventure into an odyssey of spiritual proportions. Wayne looms large in the pages of this book, particularly in chapter 2, which describes the genesis of the bicycle trip and introduces readers to Wayne, and in chapter 9, which narrates Wayne's thirty-six-hour visit with me in Fargo, North Dakota, at the midpoint of the trek. He was a great storyteller, as you may have already discovered in that chapter. Without Wayne, this book would not have been written.

As a valued visionary and a community leader, Wayne left a remarkable legacy. His three-column obituary, one of the longest ever printed in the local newspaper, indicates that in 1988 he was elected Citizen of the Year from southwestern Pennsylvania for his community activity. Wayne's involvement in the community was legendary. His untiring efforts enabled low-income individuals and other disadvantaged persons to face their situation with dignity and provided them with the resources to help themselves. He tackled head-on the ravages of hunger and drug abuse. No project was too large or too overwhelming. Through all his endeavors he set an outstanding example for others. Wayne's legacy lives on in our hearts and minds and in our resolve to dream bigger dreams and to love others—particularly those less fortunate than ourselves—with a greater passion and commitment.

Everyone knew when Wayne was in the room. At 220 pounds, he was an imposing figure, and he stood tall in those years, to his full height of six feet. He was a wonderful companion, with a warm heart, a quick wit, and a welcoming smile. His jovial personality, coupled with an air of confidence and a contagious faith, made him a formidable figure. He had a twinkle in his eyes and attractive light brown hair, and when he sported a moustache and a matching red-flecked goatee, he had a distinctive appearance.

Wayne was a charter member of Habitat for Humanity in Washington County, holding many meetings in his home. He served as vice president, treasurer, and executive director over an eight-year period, with the first house being completed in 1990.

In chapter two I relate how Wayne was stricken with an unknown muscle disorder at the age of nineteen and how that disorder advanced until he was diagnosed with muscular dystrophy. In 1977, when he was thirty-eight years old, Wayne found it impossible to perform his job as a machinist. His life changed dramatically that year, due to his premature retirement. Wayne became Mr. Mom as Peggy went to work full time to help provide the necessities of life for their two children. He found his niche as a good father, cook, babysitter, and band parent. He drove car pool to get the kids to school and even polished daughter Pam's band boots.

Over time, his forced retirement led him to deep involvement in his community. As a result, he came to view his physical debilitation not as a weakness or a setback but as a gift.

"When I was nineteen," he later affirmed, "God gave me a gift. If I hadn't had muscular dystrophy, I would never have become involved in the community." Wayne never used his disability as an excuse. He stood to his full height of six feet as he proclaimed with conviction, "We should never look at what we don't have and use it as an excuse. Rather we should look at what we do have as a gift from God and use it."

Wayne's death, as his life, was inspirational. If Wayne's style of life was "helpful"—and that's an understatement—his manner of death was "hopeful," embodying what St. Paul must have imagined when he penned those memorable words in 1 Corinthians 13:12: "For now we see in a mirror dimly, but then face to face. Now I know in part; then I shall understand fully, even as I have been fully understood."

The last months before Wayne's death had been particularly tough. Following a stay in the Intensive Care unit of the local hospital, he had become dependent on Tylenol for relief of his constant pain. The interval between pills seemed interminable. His strength was gone, and he could barely move. Bedridden, with arms tucked helplessly at his side, he was unable to complete essential chores like brushing his teeth or pulling up the covers. But during the past week, Peggy had noticed something un-usual about Wayne's condition: he had not requested any Tylenol and he seemed to be pain free. "I'm fine," he replied, refusing Peggy's offer of pain medication. Unfortunately, he was still immobile.

On the evening of April 8, 2010, the electricity went out in Wayne and Peggy Armstrong's neighborhood. It was 10:15, almost bedtime, but Peggy got a large flashlight and set it on a table, its light projecting upward toward the ceiling. Since Wayne was dependent upon an electric concen-trator to supply oxygen to a portable mask, Peggy immediately went to get an oxygen tank from the next room.

As Peggy returned with the oxygen, she hooked Wayne up and made him as comfortable as possible, for he often hyperventilated when he be-came anxious.

"Where's Sid?" Wayne asked, referring to the couple's pet Pomchi (a Pomeranian Chihuahua mix). Peggy told him he was in his cage.

"Let him out," Wayne requested. "He has better vision in the dark than we do."

Sidney promptly came over to Wayne and jumped up on the bed. Wayne spent a few minutes with the dog, petting him before asking Peggy to put him back in his cage. Peggy didn't know it yet, but Wayne was say-ing goodbye.

Wayne then asked Peggy to call 911 to let them know that he and Peggy were alone in the house without power. Peggy considered the re-quest to be excessive, so she decided, instead, to call their daughter Diana, who lived nearby.

At that point Wayne did something unexpected; he reached across his chest and grabbed a pillow, tossing it at Peggy in a playful gesture. That move got Peggy's attention, for it had been some time since Wayne had been able to extend his arms as he had just done.

After a few minutes, Wayne suddenly hollered, "Is anyone out there?" Hearing no reply, he called again, only louder. His bed was in an enclosed porch, with large plate glass windows overlooking their yard. He glanced outdoors and asked, "Who are all those people out in the yard?"

Attempting to pacify him, and without even looking outside, Peggy commented, "You're probably seeing workers from the power company."

Wayne replied, "Turn and look. They have lights."

Peggy turned around and, seeing no one, informed him that he was mistaken. "There's no one out there."

Wayne replied, "You can't see them. I can."

Though he was lying prostrate on his back, Wayne then extended both arms in the air, as though in conversation. "I can't go," he yelled. "I can't walk!"

Alarmed by this sudden outburst, Peggy pondered Wayne's emotional state, for he seemed delusional. At that point she went to check on the oxygen tank, for it had gone quiet. The tank appeared to be fine. She was relieved to hear the familiar sound as Wayne resumed breaking. There was another pause, followed by one final breath. Peggy drew closer and realized that Wayne was no longer alive. It was 12:45 a.m., April 9. That's when Peggy knew that she had witnessed something both precious and uncommon. Had Wayne departed to heaven, or had heaven invaded her home that night? Either way, eternity permeated the moment, for she felt as close to paradise as might be possible on earth.

Then grief set in. Knowing she would never be with Wayne physically again, she caressed his face and hands. As she did, she noticed that his psoriasis, a chronic skin condition, was clearing from his face and hands. She checked his chest, and noticed diminishing symptoms there as well. Peggy took this as a sign of divine grace, confirming that Wayne was heaven bound.

Peggy later mentioned that this experience was the most profound of her life, greater even than the birth of her children.

The dramatic story of Wayne's passing was told by Peggy to friends and passed on vividly to the stream of mourners who came to the William G. Neal Funeral Home to pay their respects.

On Tuesday morning, April 13, family and friends gathered at the Fourth Presbyterian Church for Wayne's funeral service. Byron Smialek, longtime columnist for the *Observer-Reporter*, Washington's daily newspaper, spoke for himself and others gathered in the sanctuary when he said: "Wayne was a better man than I; he was a better person than most of us."

"I will never forget Wayne, and what he was about," Byron continued. "In 1983, he became a charter member of '2000 Turkeys,' a program designed to raise money to feed hungry families at Thanksgiving time. It later morphed into '2000 Turkeys for the Unemployed of Washington and Greene Counties,' a name that reflected the estimated number of newly unemployed at that time, mostly steelworkers and coal miners. The donations went from $19,000 annually to $123,000, making it the single largest source of money for the Greater Washington County Food Bank. This year we hope to raise $154,000. That figure will put us over $ 1 million in total accumulated giving. We want to reach that goal in honor of Wayne Armstrong."

The Rev. Sue Kidder-Petritis, chaplain at the Washington Hospital, officiated at Wayne's funeral. Tears flowed as the congregants sang "The Old Rugged Cross," the poignant words from the final verse and the refrain seemingly penned for this occasion:

> . . . Then He'll call me someday to my home far away,
> Where His glory forever I'll share . . .
>
> So I'll cherish the old rugged cross,
> 'Till my trophies at last I lay down.
> I will cling to the old rugged cross,
> And exchange it someday for a crown.
>
> —George Bennard

"Wayne may have been challenged physically," Sue proclaimed, referring to his muscular dystrophy, "but he was never challenged spiritually. Wayne got it! When he was stricken with an unknown muscular disorder in 1960 and then with the label 'disabled,' he was not done. He was just getting started." Rev. Kidder-Petritis suggested that Wayne's epitaph might well include the farewell words attributed to Paul in 2 Timothy: "I have fought the good fight, I have finished the race, I have kept the faith" (4:7).

Thank you, Wayne, for all you have been and will ever be.

Appendix

The Merits of Road Cycling: A Personal Account

SOMETIMES I FEEL AS if I belong to an endangered species, for I am a road cyclist, and have been most of my life, ever since that day when my father took me to a rural road and relinquished his supportive hold on my bike. The training wheels were gone and I cycled unassisted for the first time, free as a bird but looking for a perch, a place to dismount. My first ride took longer than expected, for with my father far behind, I lacked the confidence to turn around or even to glance backward. My steering might have been shaky and my bicycle may have been too large, but there was nothing wrong with my balance. I just hadn't learned how to stop.

I looked ahead, determined to find some object—a stone, a stump, a step—anything to prevent me from falling when I stopped. Eventually I located a large rock by the side of the road and my joy ride came to a satisfactory conclusion. I felt pride in my accomplishment and I couldn't wait to do it again.

Growing up in the mountainous Central American nation of Costa Rica, I developed a passion for cycling. Later, in my junior high years, I biked six miles a day to an English-speaking school. Weekends meant long solo rides, with challenging hills to climb. Cycling fed my independent spirit and opened doors to a world of adventure.

Bicycle riding must have been in my blood. In the Netherlands, where my ancestors lived, bicycles are a common form of transportation. Bicycle paths are everywhere, with marked crossings, bridges, and even tunnels running parallel to most roads and highways. Cycling is as natural there as walking. In that nation of 16.5 million inhabitants, there are no school buses. Children bike to school, adults shop and ride to work on bikes, and retirees simply bike for fun and exercise.

My father was three years old when he emigrated from Holland to the United States with his family. Times were tough and before long he was helping his father with carpentry in the house-building business. He had little time to ride a bicycle as a child, and certainly did not do so during his thirty-three-year missionary career in Latin America. But after his retirement he turned to cycling for exercise and recreation, continuing this activity into his nineties. My mother, also of Dutch descent, mounted a bicycle for the first time at sixty years of age; she continued cycling on a regular basis until her death twenty-five years later.[1]

Though I biked most of my life, cycling became a routine during my midlife. Around the age of forty, when I began experiencing discomfort in my lower back, I discovered that cycling offered therapeutic benefits, when accompanied by stretching and massage. A love of sports and an obsession with exercise rekindled my dreams and sparked the passion for adventure and independence I had experienced as a child.

As a professor of religious studies, I took to heart the advice imparted by Dr. Howard J. Burnett, President of Washington and Jefferson College, to graduating seniors at the annual commencement exercises: "Life is an adventure to be lived, not a problem to be solved." Against this standard, most lives—mine included—are a contradiction.

Many of us, I trust, had exciting childhoods. I certainly did. Experiences and attitudes during my youth affirmed that life was indeed an adventure, for I understood the world to have been created by a benevolent deity for our enjoyment. As we matured, existence became more complex. In high school and college, for those of us who pursued undergraduate studies, we acquired greater intellectual sophistication. We asked a lot of questions during this interlude, and everything suddenly seemed less certain. Many of us settled down around this time, finding meaning in families and careers. I postponed these goals by enrolling in a PhD program in the field of biblical studies, thereby adding further complexity to my way of thinking. The notion that life might be an "adventure to be lived" lessened as my mindset clearly morphed into "a problem to be solved."

1. An intimate account of my parents' life, told against the background of epic change in the twentieth century, particularly in Latin America, may be found in my earlier book titled *Love Never Fails* (Mustang, OK: Tate, 2006; audio 2007).

Philosophers and theologians are known to make mountains out of foothills; attempting to clarify, they often complicate. Laymen, dizzied and disoriented by conflicting claims, frequently have trouble breathing the rarified air produced by such scholarship. Natural mountains, most majestic when visible to the senses and experienced directly, are different from spiritual mountains, which are most majestic when they remain invisible—primal, mysterious, intuitive, understated, even unstated. Spiritual mountains are meant to be mysterious; their invisibility is their greatest treasure. They are most magnificent when they remain metaphorical, when the urge to literalize them is resisted.

During midlife, with children of my own and settled into a career, I came upon the analogy of the "first and second naiveté," based on an understanding of how one reads scripture. The so-called "first naiveté" refers to the initial encounter one has with the biblical text. That initial perspective is essential, for it allows us to return to the text later, following a second stage known as the "critical state," a period of study and reflection often gained in undergraduate and graduate studies. Educated people nowadays often remain in that state, prevented by their scientific and intellectual sophistication from reading scripture or studying religion beneficially. If the journey ends there, the individual misses the third and final stage, an assimilative state called the "second naiveté" or "postcritical understanding." Bernhard W. Anderson, my biblical professor in seminary, made an analogy to this phenomenon when he wrote: "Just as the analysis of a Beethoven symphony can lead to deeper musical enjoyment of the performed work, so critical study of the Bible can lead to rereading and rehearing the biblical narrative with enhanced appreciation.[2]

As the wheel of life propelled me toward midlife, I gradually entered the "second naiveté," a postcritical phase that allowed me to integrate earlier experiences beneficially. And cycling became integral to that new perspective. In 2005, after twenty years of riding, I reached 75,000 miles, averaging nearly 4,000 miles a year. I set a lifetime goal of 100,000 miles.

During the 1990s and 2000s, as recreational and competitive cycling became more popular with the X-generation, road cycling seemed an anomaly. In 2002, for example, mountain bikes achieved industry success when they accounted for 37 percent of all bicycles sold in the US.

---

2. Bernhard W. Anderson, with Steven Bishop and Judith H. Newman, *Understanding the Old Testament*, 5th ed. (Upper Saddle River, NJ: Pearson Prentice Hall, 2007), 19.

Comfort/hybrid bikes were not far behind, at 30 percent. Those percentages continued to climb in ensuing years. Meanwhile, road bike sales represented a mere 5 percent of total sales. The reasons seemed obvious. Why should cyclists compete with unpredictable traffic, the ever-growing threat of road rage, and with drivers distracted by cell phone conversations, when off-road cycling appeared so much safer? And why expose oneself to the rigor of hills, brutal winds, and the merciless summer sun when one could bike sheltered trails on relatively flat terrain?

Road cycling, of course, is not for everyone, and even road aficionados should not pedal the pavement exclusively. But for a select core of cyclists, roadwork and touring provide significant benefits over trail cycling. The following list is limited, surely, but for me the benefits of road cycling include:

1. a greater sense of *adventure*.

   Whereas trail cycling generally leads to predictable destinations, road cycling, with its myriad riding options, always leaves the route open-ended;

2. greater *convenience*.

   In many cases roads allow one to cycle directly from home with no need for additional transportation. Hence, it is more cost effective and in this respect, more environment friendly;

3. a superior *workout*.

   Road cycling, especially on country roads such as those in western Pennsylvania and across much of the United States, requires pedaling over a hilly terrain, and hills provide a great cardiovascular workout. Regular workouts on hilly roads are the best way to lose weight and stay in shape. Cycling on recreational trails or on stationary bicycles, as many do to lose weight, rarely produces significant results. And whereas bike paths require caution due to erratic traction, slow moving pedestrians, and families on bicycles, back roads are generally safer than bike trails for speed work and cadence drills, which increase stamina and provide an exhilarating and effective workout;

4. greater *intimacy with the sport of cycling.*

    Road cycling requires better cycling skills than most trail rides. In many cases this activity encourages cyclists to perform their own bicycle maintenance, handle roadside emergencies, join a cycling club, and participate in cycling events with others. Road cycling provides a lifelong love of cycling and may open the door to competitive cycling;

5. a laboratory for *enhancing personal growth and maturity.*

    Road cycling creates experiences that provide powerful personal and emotional lessons for life, including heightened self-motivation, self control, improved decision-making abilities, strategic planning, respect for others, care for the environment, and judicious cooperation with motorists. Simply put, road cycling enhances one's conditioning, self-confidence, and self-awareness. It creates a healthy avocation, a passion for life, a concern for others, and it bestows upon the participant an ongoing sense of accomplishment.

If you have never learned how to ride a bicycle, perhaps it is not too late to start. And if it is an activity you abandoned long ago, try rekindling that childhood passion. Who knows, you may plan a vacation around cycling, ride your bike to work, or even undergo a trek of your own.